# Creative Papercrafts

# Creative Papercrafts

ANAYA PUBLISHERS LTD
LONDON

First published in Great Britain in 1994
by Anaya Publishers Ltd, Strode House,
44–50 Osnaburgh Street, London NW1 3ND

With thanks to Hilary More, Lindy Tristram and
Juliet Moxley for providing the designs in this
book.

British Library Cataloguing in Publication Data

Creative Papercrafts: 80 Projects to Make in Paper,
Papier Mâché and Découpage
  I. Title
  745.54

ISBN 1-85470-202-5

Typeset by Servis Filmsetting Ltd, Manchester, UK
Printed and bound in Hong Kong

# Contents

# Introduction

*Creating with paper is fun, easy and inexpensive. This book brings together a wealth of ideas for découpage, papier mâché and general paper decorations which all ages will enjoy making.*

For centuries paper has been used as a decorative material. This book brings together two of the most popular of papercrafts, découpage and papier mâché, along with stylish party decorations.

The projects in *Creative Papercrafts* are simple to make yet stylish and decorative, appealing to all ages and can easily be made at home with only a few pieces of equipment.

The book is divided into four chapters – Découpage, Papier mâché, Party decorations and Better Techniques. Before starting any projects, read the Better Techniques section as all the methods used in the book are explained in detail here.

Basic tools and equipment are described, and you will also find useful information on choosing materials and helpful hint on how to achieve a perfect result every time.

### Découpage
Découpage became popular during the 18th century, inspired by the elaborate lacquer furniture that was coming to Europe from China and Japan. The Victorians embraced the craft with enthusiasm and it quickly became a fashionable pastime.

The great advantage of découpage is that, unlike other art forms, you do not need to be able to draw to achieve a stunning result. Découpage shapes are carefully cut out and stuck down on another object in an attractive arrangement, then sealed with several coats of hard-wearing varnish.

Nowadays, the craft has been taken one step further with the introduction of all sorts of unusual paint and varnish finishes which emphasize the shapes while adding a new dimension.

### Suitable surfaces
Découpage works well on most surfaces but is traditionally associated with wood. It is the perfect surface for a variety of different finishes, and there is a huge range of paints, stains and coloured varnishes, which can be painted, sponged, spattered or dabbed. With the specialist paints and varnishes widely available today, wood can also be limed, given a granite effect or aged.

Alternatively, you can leave the work untreated, simply covering it with varnish to seal and give a gloss finish to the untreated areas of wood.

You can also apply découpage to china, plastic, cork or another paper. Before adding stuck-on shapes to a surface, check that it can support the dampening effect of pasted paper and then layers of varnish.

Choose your découpage shapes first, as their style and colour will determine the treatment to use. Start collecting paper cut outs, old cards, labels, sweet wrappers, magazines and stickers, to transform objects around your home and create treasured gifts for your family and friends.

## Papier mâché

The French were the first Europeans to develop papier mâché in the 18th century. The craft was particularly popular in the 1800s and was used to make a wide range of products from small bowls to tables and chairs.

The craft had almost completely died out by the early 20th century, but today it is enjoying a revival as a recycling craft. The old techniques of working paper and paste into a useful fabric are updated with modern adhesives. Quick-drying and easy-to-use acrylic paints make the final decoration easy to do.

## Basic techniques

There are two basic techniques in this book. The first, layering, involves pasting pieces of paper over a mould to form a shell and then the mould is removed. This technique is used to make projects like the bowls and Easter hen. Layering is also used to cover a permanent structure or framework which is afterwards decorated, like the black and white cat.

The other basic technique uses paper pulp. This is used to cover a basic structure, such as cardboard and is also used for modelling. The man-in-the-moon is an example of this method.

Mixed wallpaper paste is used in the papier mâché projects in this book, however, this contains a fungicide which you may not want your children to work with. If this is so, use flour and water paste, a recipe for this is also given. Alternatively, use a ready-made water-soluble paste which can be bought from craft shops.

Many of the ideas in this book are true re-cycling projects, making full use of throw-away materials. Brown paper bags and newspaper-stuffed plastic shopping bags have been transformed into toy bears, cats and ducks. Pulp egg cartons make a set of pretty egg-cups; the thin cardboard of cerial packets has been used for a number of structures and cartons discarded by supermarkets are an excellent source of corrugated card and strong, rigid cardboard.

Papier mâché is a lot of fun to do, and in no time at all, you will be developing the craft in your own way and go on to create even more exciting and beautiful things from just paper, card and paste.

# Enamel jug

*Smarten up a plain white enamel jug with a coat of metal paint and a handful of quick-to-use floral and butterfly decals – you'll be amazed at the transformation!*

### Materials
Plain enamel jug
Metal paint (Hammerite)
Floral and butterfly decals
PVA adhesive
Clear gloss varnish
Fine glasspaper

### Preparation
**1** Give the enamel jug a generous coat of metal paint (Hammerite), being careful to finish the paint neatly round the top of the jug. Leave to dry for several weeks.

Use several coats of metal paint to cover the enamel jug and leave to dry thoroughly.

### Planning the arrangement
**2** Cut the decals from the sheets, trimming them as necessary. Lay them out on a flat surface and decide their position on the jug. Using PVA adhesive, stick the decals over the jug in your chosen arrangement. Leave to dry.

After deciding on the spacing, stick the decals on to the jug, using PVA adhesive.

### Finishing
**3** Give the jug several coats of varnish, leaving it to dry between each one. Lightly sand down the jug with glasspaper between the final coats.

### Using the jug
The découpaged jug can be used and washed afterwards, but wash and dry it carefully.

# Vase

*With the clever art of glass découpage, you can turn a plain glass vase into a painted masterpiece, attractive enough to be the centre of attention in any room.*

### Materials
Plain glass vase, with a top large enough for a hand to fit inside
Floral giftwrap paper
Putty adhesive (Blu-tak)
Chinagraph pencil
PVA adhesive
Water-based household or craft paint and small natural sponge
Clear varnish (optional)

### Preparation
1 Clean the vase both inside and out and dry thoroughly.

### Marking the design
2 Choose and carefully cut out the flower heads from the giftwrap paper. To decide on the best arrangement, secure the flower heads inside the vase against the glass with a small piece of putty adhesive (Blu-tak). When you are happy with the arrangement, mark the design on the right side of the glass with the chinagraph pencil. Carefully remove the flower heads from inside the vase.

### Fixing the flowers in position
3 Dilute the PVA adhesive with a little water. Coat the front of each flower liberally with the PVA and press their right sides against the glass on the inside of the vase in each marked position. Make sure that you smooth out any air bubbles. Wipe away any excess PVA with a clean damp cloth, to keep the vase clean. Leave to dry.

### Painting the vase
4 Before you paint the vase check that all the edges of each flower are stuck firmly to the glass, otherwise the paint will seep under the edges of the paper.

5 Use the sponge and a dabbing motion to apply paint all over the inside of the vase and paper shapes. Leave to dry. When the paint has dried, add a second layer of paint making sure that no patches of glass can be seen. Leave to dry.

6 If wished, the inside of the vase can be given a coat of varnish. Remove all the chinagraph marks from the outside.

Draw round the decal on the right side of the glass, using a chinagraph pencil.

### Holding flowers
The completed vase will not stand up to water. If you want the vase to hold fresh flowers, slip another tin or smaller vase inside the decorated vase and use this to hold the flowers.

# Tea tray

*Brighten up a plain wooden tray with a pretty wallpaper border
and a touch of matching paint to make it smart
enough for any occasion.*

### Materials
Plain wooden tray
Masking tape
Matt household or craft paint
Roll of wallpaper border
Soft pencil, ruler, set square and eraser
PVA adhesive
Clear gloss varnish
Fine glasspaper

### Preparation
**1** Wipe over the tray to remove dust and finger marks. Stick masking tape along the top edge on the inside and outside of the tray. Stick masking tape round the hand holes in the same way.

**2** Using a fine artists' paint brush, carefully paint round the top edge of the tray and round the inside of each handle hole. Leave to dry. Add a second coat if necessary. Remove masking tape.

### Marking border strips' position
**3** Decide on the position of the border on the tray base. Use a soft pencil and ruler to mark out a rectangle in the base of the tray. This will be the position of the border strips.

**4** Cut a strip of wallpaper border to fit each side of the rectangle. Carefully cut round the design along the edge of each border strip.

### Sticking the strips
**5** Coat the back of the first strip with PVA adhesive and stick in position following the marks. Stick on the next strip. Mark across the corner using the set square for a perfect diagonal. Cut along the marked line. Fold back the

corner and trim the underneath strip so it is ¼in (6mm) longer. Add some more adhesive and smooth over the corner to form the mitre.

**6** Repeat, cutting and sticking the remaining strips in position to complete the rectangle. Leave to dry.

### Finishing
**7** Rub off any pencil marks. Give the whole tray several coats of varnish, leaving it to dry between coats. Lightly sand down between the final coats.

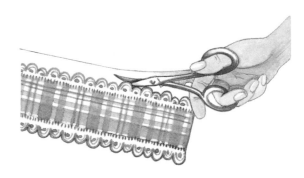

Carefully cut round the printed border, using a pair of manicure scissors if necessary.

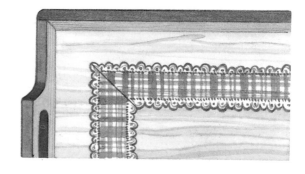

Add more adhesive and smooth over the corner to form the mitre.

# Flowered mirror

*Transform an old mirror and frame into a flowery masterpiece complete with gold outline.*

**Materials**
Tracing paper
Floral giftwrap paper
White typing paper
Mirror in frame
Spray adhesive and cleaning fluid
Spray gold paint
PVA adhesive
Small self-adhesive stickers
Clear gloss varnish
Fine glasspaper

**Making the leaf stencil**
1  To make the leaf stencil, trace off one leaf from the floral giftwrap paper. Cut a piece of typing paper the exact size of the mirror inside the frame. Mark 5 leaf motifs round the top right-hand corner of the paper. Cut out each leaf stencil.

2  Using spray adhesive, stick the stencilled paper exactly over the mirror.

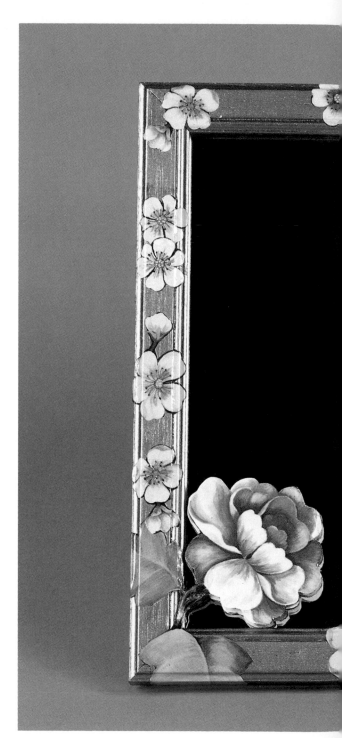

Choose a giftwrap paper with a distinctive open flower head design for the large flower.

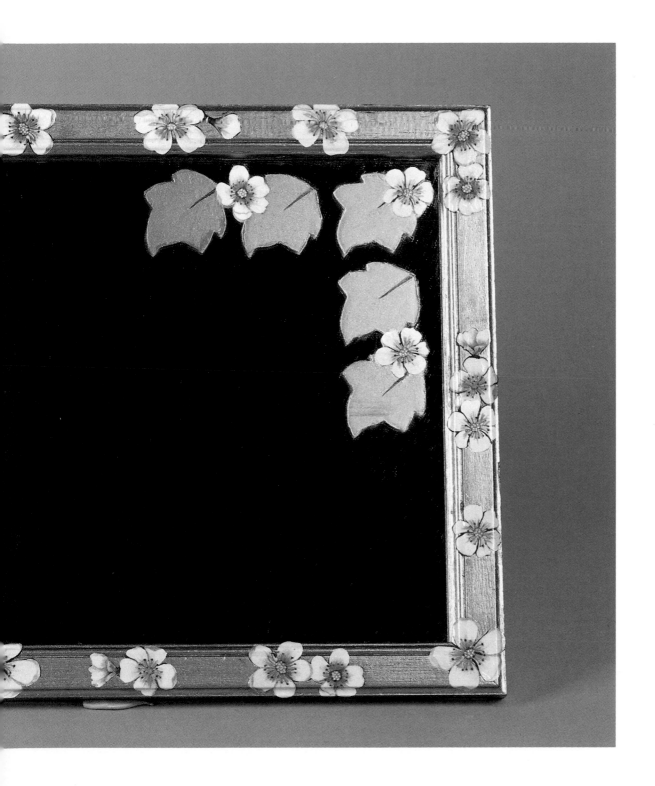

**3** Spray the mirror frame with 2 good coats of gold paint. Leave to dry.

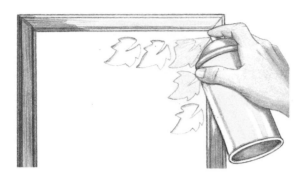

Spray the mirror frame with 2 coats of gold paint, and leave to dry thoroughly.

**4** Carefully remove the stencil and clean the adhesive residue off the mirror with cleaning fluid.

Stick flower heads randomly round the outside of the frame and to the stencilled leaves.

### Making the floral decoration

**5** Cut out small flower heads from the giftwrap paper. Using PVA adhesive, stick flower heads haphazardly round the outside of the frame and to the leaf stencils on the mirror, leaving the bottom left-hand corner free.

**6** Roughly cut out 3 large flower heads and 1 large flower head complete with stalk and leaves. Use spray adhesive to stick the flower heads plus the flower head of the flower with leaves on to white paper. Carefully cut out each piece.

**7** Use one of the self-adhesive stickers to stick one flower head in the left-hand corner of the mirror. Stick the remaining large flower heads exactly over the first one with a self-adhesive sticker between each one.

Stick on the large flower head, with the outer petals touching the edge of the frame.

### Using real leaves

As an alternative to tracing round leaves printed on giftwrap paper, you can collect real leaves from your garden or local park, and use them as the basis for your stencil. Simply proceed as before, but lay the leaves on a piece of white paper before tracing them.

Choose flat, medium-sized or large leaves, according to the size of your mirror, or you can use two or three leaves, of different sizes. Leaves with an interesting outline, such as many of the Japanese maples, are ideal, and can create a delicate, Oriental look. Remember, though, the more intricate the outline, the longer it takes to cut the shape out, and the more patience is needed.

**8** Finally stick on the flower head with leaves, so the head is level with the frame edge. Carefully take the stalk and leaves and stick them round the frame with PVA adhesive.

Stick on the flower head with leaves, then stick the stalk and leaves round the frame.

**Finishing**
**9** Carefully paint the frame, stencilled motifs and large flower head with varnish. Leave to dry. Add several more coats of varnish, lightly sanding down the frame between the final coats.

---

**Mirror additions**
If you prefer not to use a spray gold paint, the mirror can be treated with Liquid Leaf metallic paint. Draw up the stencil in the same way as before and stick over the mirror. Then use a brush to cover the frame with the gold paint. To use the stencil, pour a little of the paint into a saucer and, using a natural sponge, dab over the stencil to mark it on to the mirror. Leave to dry and repeat. When the second coat is dry, remove the stencil and continue as before.

---

# Waste paper bin

*Give your rubbish a floral send off with this decorated waste paper bin. Use an off-cut of wallpaper border and match it up to the decorations in the rest of the bedroom.*

## Materials
Masking tape
Metal waste paper bin
Pale green spray paint
Wallpaper border
PVA adhesive
Clear gloss varnish
Fine glasspaper

## Preparation
1 Use masking tape to mask off the top rim of the bin. Paint the bin pale green with 2 coats of spray paint, leaving it to dry well before adding the second coat.

## Decorating the bin
2 Measure round the top and base edges of the bin and cut 2 border strips from the wallpaper border. Using PVA adhesive, carefully stick the strips in place, trimming ends so they butt together.

3 Carefully cut out several large flower motifs from the border strip. Coat with PVA and stick centrally round the bin, overlapping one group with the next, to provide a continuous design.

Stick flower motifs centrally round the bin, overlapping one group with the next.

## Varnishing
4 Give the bin several coats of varnish, leaving it to dry between each coat. Lightly sand down the bin with glasspaper between the final coats.

Stick a border strip round the top and base edges, using PVA adhesive.

# Flower pots

*Even plain flower pots can be given a new lease of life if they are cleaned up and decorated with a simple palm tree motif. Then they are ready to hold your favourite plants.*

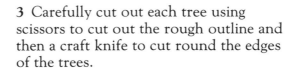

**Materials**
PVA adhesive
Flower pots, about 4in (10cm) high
Tracing paper
Green corrugated paper
Clear gloss varnish

**Sealing the pots**
1 Dilute some PVA adhesive to the consistency of thin cream and paint over the outside and inside of the flower pots to seal them. Leave the flower pots to dry before decorating them.

**Making the motif**
2 Trace off the palm tree motif (see below). Mark on to the wrong side of the corrugated paper with the lines of the paper going lengthways up the tree. Mark out 4 trees for each flower pot you want to decorate.

3 Carefully cut out each tree using scissors to cut out the rough outline and then a craft knife to cut round the edges of the trees.

**Sticking the trees in place**
4 Use full strength PVA to stick each tree in place round the pot, spacing them evenly apart.

Stick the palm trees, evenly spaced apart, to the pot, using full strength PVA adhesive.

**Finishing**
5 Paint over the whole pot with diluted PVA to create a seal and give the pot a shine. Leave to dry.

6 Paint the pots with a 2 coats of varnish, leaving the pot to dry between each coat.

Trace this simple palm tree motif and transfer it to a piece of corrugated paper.

# Storage canisters

*Whether they are glass, enamel or tin, storage canisters can be given added sparkle with pretty paper cut outs, making them an attractive addition to your kitchen.*

**Materials**
Storage tins
Cake frill
PVA adhesive
Floral wallpaper
Clear gloss varnish
Fine glasspaper

**Making the frill**
1 Measure round the widest part of each tin and cut a length of cake frill the same measurement plus 1in (2.5cm). Cut 2 lengths of cake frill, if wished.

2 Coat the frill with PVA adhesive and stick it round the tin, trimming off excess to make a neat join.

**Making the flowers**
3 Carefully cut out flowers from the floral wallpaper. Coat the backs with PVA and stick them to the tin, overlapping the cake frill or frills. Cut out and stick a motif in the centre of the lid in the same way.

Stick the flower decals on to the tin, overlapping the cake frill or frills.

**Varnishing**
4 Give the tin several coats of varnish, leaving it to dry between each coat. Lightly sand down with glasspaper between the final coats.

Stick the cake frills round the tin, top and bottom, trimming off excess to make them fit.

# Musical clock

*To help you keep in time with the music. Old sheets of music are torn into pieces which are then stuck on a cork place mat to create an unusual clock.*

## Materials
Round cork table mat
Drill and bit to fit clock hands
Spray fixative
4 sheets of music
PVA adhesive
Clear gloss varnish
Clear adhesive
Fine glasspaper
4 red beads and 8 black beads
Clock hands, mechanism and battery

## Preparation
1 Drill a hole in the centre of the cork mat large enough to fit in the clock mechanism.

2 Spray fixative over both sides of each sheet of music. Roughly tear the sheets into long strips.

3 Dilute the PVA adhesive with water to the consistency of thin cream and paint over the front of the cork table mat to seal it. Leave to dry.

## Sticking on the decoration
4 Using PVA, stick the strips of music to the cork, sticking them in a random fashion, overlapping each one. Continue until the cork is covered, keeping the central hole open.

5 Take the strips over the outer edge to the wrong side of the cork mat and trim to form a ½in (13mm) border all round. Paint over the whole front with diluted PVA and leave to dry.

## Varnishing
6 Give the clock several coats of varnish, leaving it to dry between each one. Lightly sand down between the final coats.

## Fixing clock mechanism
7 Use clear adhesive to stick the large red beads at the 12, 3, 6 and 9 o'clock positions. Stick the smaller black beads at 5-minute intervals in between the red beads.

8 Fix the clock hands in position in the central hole and insert the battery into the mechanism at the back of the clock.

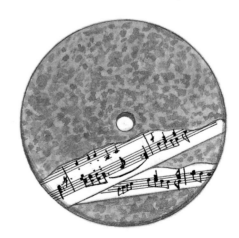

Stick the strips of sheet music to the cork mat, randomly and slightly overlapping.

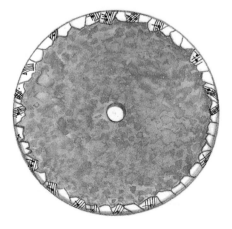

Continue the strips over the edge and trim to form a ½in (1cm) border all the way round.

### Timely options

You could use the same technique to get a softer, more feminine effect by substituting strips from two different patterns of floral giftwrap paper, with the same or similar colourways.

For a teenager's room or modern kitchen, use strips torn from bold, geometric giftwrap paper. And for a subtle effect, tear strips of solid-colour art papers, in tints and shades of the same hue: pale, mid- and deep blue, for example, or pinks and reds. You may need to use gold or silver beads and clock hands, to show up against rich or dark colours.

# Sewing box

*Transform a plain wooden box into a glamorous sewing box by giving it a limed sheen, then decorate with sewing motifs made from button samples cut from a catalogue.*

**Materials**
Large whitewood trinket/sewing box
Wire wool and wire brush
White emulsion paint
White spirit
Liming wax
Clean soft cloth
Button catalogue
PVA adhesive
Clear gloss varnish
Fine glasspaper

**Liming the box**
1 Rub over the outside of the box with wire wool and the wire brush to raise the grain. Wipe over with a wet cloth to remove any residue.

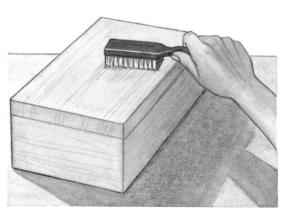

Use the wire brush to raise the grain on the top and sides of the wooden box.

2 Paint over the box with white emulsion and leave to dry. Wipe over the whole box with white spirit to remove the excess white paint; it will remain in the cracks and grain lines. Leave to dry.

3 Rub over the whole box with liming wax and buff to a faint sheen with a clean soft cloth.

4 Carefully cut out the buttons from the catalogue, choosing ones with a distinctive colour and shape. Arrange the buttons at random over the lid of the box.

**Decorating with buttons**
5 Dilute the PVA adhesive with a little water, then use it to stick the buttons on to the lid of the box in a haphazard arrangement. Overlap the buttons with each other and mix up the colours and shapes. Smooth over each button to eliminate any air bubbles and to make sure it is well stuck down.

6 Following the same process, stick a few buttons at random on the front of the box, on each side and along the back. Leave to dry.

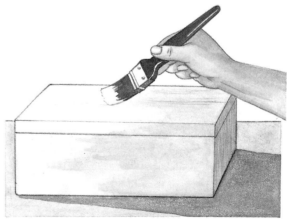

Paint over the box with white emulsion paint and then leave to dry.

## Finishing the box

**7** Give the box several coats of varnish, leaving it to dry between each one. Lightly sand down with glasspaper between the final coats.

**Decorating the inside of the box**
To decorate the inside of the box, either paint it or lime the wood in the same way as the outside, or line it with pretty fabric or felt.

# Glass plate

*Wrappers from your favourite sweets provide coloured foil to turn into pretty plate decorations. Cut out old-fashioned 'snowflake' patterns to create the shapes.*

### Materials
10in (25cm) diameter glass plate
Selection of coloured foil papers
Spray adhesive
Liquid Leaf
Treasure Sealer

### Preparation
1  Clean the plate thoroughly to remove any greasy marks.

### Cutting 'snowflake' patterns
2  Smooth out the foil sweet papers. Cut each piece into a square, by folding up one edge diagonally until it meets the opposite edge. Trim off the excess. Unfold.

3  Take each square and fold in half, then into quarters and then into eighths. Snip off the centre point. Cut out small V shapes in all the sides of the folded foil. Carefully unfold the 'snowflake' design. Cut as many squares as necessary for covering the plate.

### Attaching the patterns
4  Turn the plate over. Spray adhesive on the back of the plate. Overlap smaller squares all round the outer edge.

5  Place the foil motifs over the centre of the back of the plate, overlapping each one until the whole area has been covered. When the entire back of the plate has been covered with foil motifs leave it to dry.

### Finishing the plate
6  Use a brush to paint the Liquid Leaf over the back of the plate. Leave to dry and add a second coat if necessary.

7  Trim round the edge of the plate and paint with Liquid Leaf to create a smooth finish. Then coat with a layer of sealer.

Cut out small V shapes along each edge of the diagonally folded foil sweet paper.

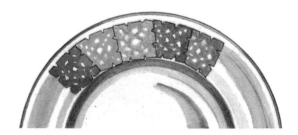

Overlap smaller squares all round the outer edge, then leave to dry thoroughly.

**Display ideas**
Hang the plate, or a trio of decorated
glass plates, on a plain wall, or use
the plate for serving sweets wrapped
in coloured foil papers similar to the
ones used – ideal for a children's
party or Christmas festivities.

# Jewellery box

*The perfect gift for friends. They can keep all their favourite jewellery together in one pretty box, which is crackle painted and then covered in stylized fruit.*

**Materials**
Small whitewood trinket box
Yellow emulsion paint
Decal-it
Crackle-it
Artists' oil paint in raw umber
Giftwrap paper with fruit motifs
PVA adhesive
Clear gloss varnish
Fine glasspaper

**Preparation**
1 Prime the box as necessary, then paint with yellow emulsion paint and leave to dry.

2 Coat the box with a thick coat of Decal-it and leave to dry. Then paint on Crackle-it and leave to dry.

3 When the box is dry, use a clean cloth to rub raw umber paint into the cracks that have appeared on the box. Rub off excess paint.

**Decorating**
4 Choose the fruit motifs from the giftwrap paper and carefully cut out. Using PVA adhesive, stick the motifs over the box. Leave to dry.

**Varnishing**
5 Give the box several coats of varnish, leaving the box to dry between each one. Lightly sand down the box between the final coats.

Rub raw umber paint into the cracks that appear in the paint, using a soft cloth.

Stick the fruit motifs over the box, using PVA adhesive, and leave to dry.

# Photograph frame

*Surround photographs of loved ones in this simple wooden frame, beautifully decorated with bright flower heads stuck one above the other all round the frame.*

**Materials**
Plain wooden photograph frame
PVA adhesive
Sheet of flower decals
Gold paint or gold pen
Clear gloss varnish
Fine glasspaper

**Preparation**
**1** Remove the backing and glass from the frame and leave to one side. Dilute the PVA adhesive with a little water to consistency of thin cream and paint it, using long, even strokes, over the frame to seal the wood.

**Attaching the flowers**
**2** Cut the decals from their mount. Using PVA adhesive, stick the decals on to the frame. Keep the flower heads the right way up on the sides, base and top of the mirror frame.

**3** Stick more decals round the sides of the frame and merge the 2 sets together. Leave to dry.

**Painting the border**
**4** Using a sharp craft knife and ruler, carefully trim round the inner edge of the frame, leaving a $\frac{1}{8}$in (3mm) wide border of frame showing. Paint the border gold and leave to dry.

**Finishing**
**5** Give the frame several coats of varnish, leaving it to dry between each one. Lightly sand down between the final coats.

**6** Replace the backing and glass in the mirror frame.

Stick the decals on to the frame, keeping the flower heads the right way up.

Carefully trim round the inner edge of the frame, leaving an $\frac{1}{8}$in (3mm) wide border.

# Trinket boxes

*Trinket boxes are perfect for gifts, and can be used to hold rings and other tiny items. Create different effects with a variety of paint and varnishes, then add cut-out motifs or decals.*

### ROSE-COVERED BOX
**Materials**
Rose decals
PVA adhesive
Small whitewood box
Clear gloss varnish
Fine glasspaper

**Decorating the box lid**
**1** Carefully remove the rose decals from their sheets. Using PVA adhesive, stick the roses on to the box lid, overlapping them in an attractive arrangement. Leave to dry.

Stick the rose decals on to the box lid, overlapping them attractively.

**Varnishing the box**
**2** Coat the box in several coats of varnish, leaving it to dry between each coat. Lightly sand down the box between the final coats.

**Decals**
**3** Decals are available in a variety of sizes and shapes, such as the daisy design pictured on the far right.

## CRACKLE PAINTED BOX
### Materials
Small whitewood box
Blue and white emulsion paints
Gum arabic
Floral giftwrap paper
PVA adhesive
Clear gloss varnish
Fine glasspaper

### Preparation
**1** Prime the box as necessary and then paint with blue emulsion paint. Leave to dry. When the paint is dry, coat the whole box in gum arabic and leave to dry again.

**2** Using a large brush, paint on the white paint, painting across the box and lid in one stroke. Do not go over any section that has already been painted white. Leave the box to dry and cracks will appear.

**3** If the cracks look too large, paint over with another coat of gum arabic and then another coat of white emulsion paint. Leave the box to dry between the different coats.

### Decorating the box
**4** Use a fine brush to paint a narrow band of blue paint round the base and top of the box base.

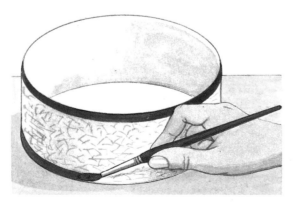

Paint a narrow band of blue round the base and top of the box base.

**5** Carefully cut out floral motifs from the giftwrap paper. Using PVA, stick the motifs on the box lid. Leave to dry.

### Varnishing
**6** Give the box several coats of varnish, leaving it to dry between each coat. Lightly sand down between the final coats.

## FLOWER BOX
### Materials
Floral giftwrap paper
PVA adhesive
Tiny whitewood box
Clear gloss varnish
Fine glasspaper

### Decorating the box
**1** Carefully cut out flower heads from the giftwrap paper.

Stick the flower heads all over the box and lid and leave to dry thoroughly.

**2** Using PVA adhesive, stick the flower heads all over the tiny box and lid until it is totally covered. Leave to dry.

### Varnishing
**3** Give the box several coats of varnish, leaving it to dry between coats. Lightly sand down between the final coats.

## SPARKLING BOX
### Materials
Tiny whitewood box
Sparkling Sandstones in Dark Jadeite
Floral giftwrap paper
PVA adhesive
Clear gloss varnish

### Painting the box
1 Paint the box with 2 coats of Sparkling Sandstones, leaving it to dry completely between the coats.

### Decorating the lid
2 Carefully cut out a flower motif from the giftwrap paper. Using PVA adhesive, stick the flower motif on to the lid of the box. Leave to dry.

### Varnishing
3 Give the box several coats of varnish, leaving it to dry between coats.

> **Tips on painting with textured acrylic paint (sparkling sandstones).**
> ● Stir the paint vigorously to mix well before use.
> ● Paint in 2 layers using a cross-hatch method – paint one way and then in the opposite direction.
> ● Different colours can be mixed together.
> ● The brushes can be cleaned in water.

# Hat box

*An old-fashioned hat box decorated with beautiful flowers and fruit makes the perfect place to store love letters, old photographs (or your favourite hat).*

### Materials
Flat-packet hat box
Giftwrap paper with flowers and fruit
PVA adhesive
Clear gloss varnish
Fine glasspaper

### Preparation
**1** Make up the hat box, sticking any sections together for a sturdy construction.

### Arranging the decoration
**2** Select the motifs from the giftwrap paper. Carefully cut out each flower following the outline. Cut out a selection of fruit in the same way.

**3** Arrange a still life on the lid of the box, grouping together flowers and fruit. When you have the result you want stick them in place with PVA adhesive.

### Finishing
**4** Cut 3 flower or leaf motifs for each side of the box. Using PVA, stick each motif in position, checking that it will not be obscured by the closed lid before you secure it.

**5** Give the hat box several coats of varnish, leaving it to dry between coats. Lightly sand down between the final coats of varnish.

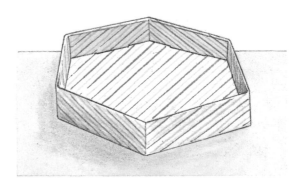

Make up the hat box, sticking the sections together as directed.

Arrange a still life, using the flower and fruit cut-outs, on the box lid.

### Design touch
As well as hat boxes, inexpensive, flat-pack boxes come in a variety of shapes, sizes and plain or patterned surfaces – ideal for storing sweaters or out-of-season clothes. Use the fruit and flower shapes, or motifs of your choice, to decorate several different boxes, for a coordinated, 'designer' look.

# Candlestick and candle

*Dinner by candle-light will be enhanced with an attractive sponged candlestick holding a candle decorated with designs cut from silver and gold doileys.*

**Materials**
Red and silver matt craft paint
Gold stained wooden candlestick
Small natural sponges
Spray fixative
Gold and silver doileys
PVA adhesive
Clear gloss varnish
Red candle to fit the candlestick

**Decorating the candlestick**
**1** Pour a small amount of red paint into a saucer and a small amount of silver paint into another saucer. Dip one sponge into the red paint. Dab the excess on to a sheet of kitchen towel and then dab all over the candlestick. Leave to dry.

Using a natural sponge, dab silver paint all over the candlestick.

**2** Then dab all over the candlestick with silver paint in the same way.

**3** Repeat steps 1 and 2 once more until the candlestick has a mottled effect. Leave to dry.

**4** Spray fixative over the doileys. Carefully cut out motifs from the doileys, reserving some for the candle. Dilute the PVA adhesive with a little water and use to stick the motifs over the candlestick. Leave to dry.

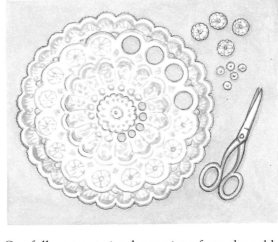

Carefully cut out circular sections from the gold and silver doileys.

**5** Give the candlestick several coats of varnish, leaving it to dry between each one.

**Decorating the candle**
**6** Gently heat the back of a teaspoon and press on to the candle. Press the reserved cut-out doiley motifs into the melted wax. Repeat to add motifs all round the candle.

# Table mats

*Clever stamping with an ink stamp and pad can produce brightly-coloured shapes that can be quickly cut out and stuck to plain cork mats to make them look special.*

**Materials**
Cork table mats
Enamel paint
Ink stamp of dragonfly and butterfly
Ink pad for stamp
White cartridge paper
Spray fixative
PVA adhesive
Clear gloss varnish
Fine glasspaper

**Preparation**
1 Paint the mats with enamel paint.
Leave to dry.

**Making the decoration**
2 Using the ink stamps and pad, mark a series of dragonflies and butterflies on the white paper. Spray with fixative.
Carefully cut round each motif.

3 Using PVA adhesive, stick the motifs in place all over the mats in a haphazard arrangement. Leave to dry.

Using PVA adhesive, stick the motifs in place all over the mats in a haphazard arrangement.

**Varnishing**
4 Cover each mat in several coats of varnish, leaving them to dry between each coat. Lightly sand down between the final coats.

Stamp a series of dragonflies and butterflies on the white paper, using an ink stamp and pad.

# Lamp with shade

*Give a sophisticated new look to a plain white table lamp and shade by decorating them with smart black and white butterfly motifs cut from photocopies.*

## Materials
Lampshade and base
Masking tape
Black fabric paint
Photocopies of animal or insect motifs in
   two different sizes from a book or
   magazine (see below)
PVA adhesive
Clear gloss varnish

## Preparing the shade
**1** Use tape to mask off the top and base bindings round the shade. Carefully paint the top and base bindings with black fabric paint. Leave to dry.

**2** If necessary, paint round the bindings again once the first coat has dried. Make sure that the paint is taken inside the frame to provide a good outline. When the paint is dry, peel off the masking tape.

## Applying the motifs
**3** Carefully cut round each of the photocopied motifs.

**4** Wipe over the lamp base to make sure it is clean and dry. Using PVA adhesive, stick motifs to the shade. Then stick motifs to the lamp base.

Stick motifs, well spaced out, to the shade and base, using PVA adhesive.

**5** Paint over the shade and base with 2 coats of varnish, leaving them to dry between coats.

> **Note:** The varnish may slightly change the colour of the fabric of the shade, as well as slightly rough up the surface of the fabric.

Using black fabric paint, carefully paint the top and base bindings.

> **Number of motifs**
> The number of photocopied motifs you need for decorating your lamp will depend on the size of the lamp and shade you are découpaging and the size of the motifs you are photocopying from a book or magazine.

# Stationery rack

*Keep all your writing paper, envelopes and letters neatly together in one place in this brightly-painted rack covered in smart stickers of your choice.*

**Materials**
Stationery rack
White spray paint
Yellow enamel paint
Self-adhesive stickers in various designs
   and numbers
Clear gloss varnish
Fine glasspaper

**Painting the rack**
1  Spray paint the whole rack with white paint and leave to dry. Repeat with a second coat as necessary.

2  Carefully paint the side edges, the base and along the top of each partition with yellow paint. Leave to dry.

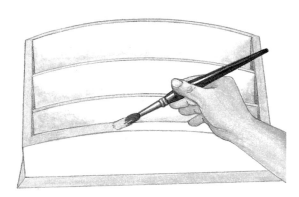

Using yellow paint, paint the side and partition edges and base, then leave to dry.

**Sticker themes**
There are so many attractive stickers available that you could personalize the stationery rack: fish for a keen fisherman, zodiac signs for an avid astrologer or panda bears for a budding naturalist.

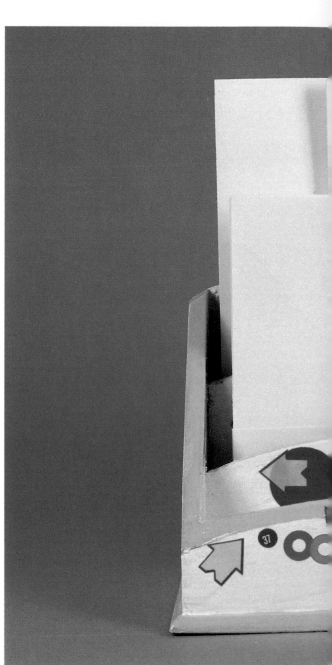

## Finishing the rack

**3** Peel off the stickers and stick at random over the whole rack, inside and out.

**4** Give the rack several coats of varnish, leaving it to dry between each one. Lightly sand down between the final coats.

Stick self-adhesive stickers randomly over the stationary rack, inside and out.

# Ash tray

*Smart glass ash trays can be ornamental as well as practical. This one is definitely ornamental with its sea shell design made from cut-out giftwrap and sponged paints.*

### Materials
Sea shell giftwrap paper
PVA adhesive
Small square glass ash tray
Blue and green matt paints
2 natural sponges
Clear gloss varnish

### Sticking on the motifs
**1** Carefully cut out 5 sea shell shapes from the giftwrap paper. Using PVA adhesive, stick the motifs to the outside of the ash tray, placing one in the centre of the base and one on each of the 4 sides. Leave to dry.

Turn the ash tray upside down and dab with green and then blue paint.

Cut out 5 sea shell motifs and stick one on each side of the ash tray and one in the centre.

### Painting the ash tray
**2** Stand the ash tray upside down, with the base uppermost. Pour a little green paint into a saucer. Dip the sponge into the paint and dab on to a sheet of kitchen paper to remove the excess paint, then dab paint all over the base of the ash tray. Leave to dry.

**3** Pour some blue paint into another saucer. Use a clean sponge to dab paint all over the base of the ash tray in the same way as before. Leave to dry.

**4** Repeat steps 2 and 3 as necessary until there is a good mottled effect over the base of the ash tray. Leave to dry before varnishing.

**5** Give the ash tray 2 coats of clear gloss varnish, leaving it to dry completely between each coat.

# Pencil tub and note box

*Recycle old stamps by using them to brighten up a dull desk set. Create a pencil tub and matching note box that will look smart in any work station.*

## Materials

Used postage stamps
Blotting or kitchen paper
PVA adhesive
Tub or clean tin suitable for pencils
Note box
Clear gloss varnish
Fine glasspaper
Self-adhesive felt

## Preparation

1 If necessary soak the stamps off old
envelopes and postcards. Fill a bowl of
warm water, drop in the envelopes and
leave for a few minutes; the stamps will
float off. Leave to dry on blotting or
kitchen paper.

2 Dilute the PVA adhesive with water to
the consistency of thin cream. Paint a
thin layer over the tub, inside and out.
Leave to dry.

## Decorating the tub

3 Beginning on the outside, use PVA
adhesive to stick stamps over the whole
of the outside of the tub, pasting the
stamps at an angle, each one overlapping
the one before. At the top edge, take the
stamps over the rim for about ⅜in (1cm).
Treat the base edge in the same way.
Smooth out all round the tub. Paint with
a thin coat of diluted PVA and leave to
dry.

Stick used postage stamps over the whole of the
outside of the tub, using PVA adhesive.

4 Stick stamps over the inside of the tub
but in regular rows, covering the edges of
the outside stamps. Coat with diluted
PVA as before and leave to dry.

Stick stamps in regular rows over the inside,
overlapping the outside stamps.

## Finishing the tub

5 Paint the inside and outside of the tub
with several coats of varnish, leaving the
tub to dry in between each coat. Lightly
sand down between the final coats.

6 Stand the tub on the paper side of the
felt and mark round it. Cut out ¼in
(6mm) inside the marked outline. Peel off
the protective coating and stick the felt to
the base, covering the edges of the
stamps.

## Decorating the note box

7 Cover the note box in the same way as
the tub. At the corners, snip into the
stamps up to the box and tuck in the
excess, so each corner will remain sharp.
Cut and stick on a felt base in the same
way.

# School file

*Smarten up boring school files and notebooks with simple letters cut out of wrappers from your favourite chocolate and sweet bars.*

**Materials**
White typing paper
Spray adhesive
Paper wrappers from chocolate and sweet bars
Stencils of letters in different sizes
PVA adhesive
File and/or notebook
Spray fixative

**Making the letters**
1 Mark a straight line across the white typing paper. Using spray adhesive, stick the wrappers in a diagonal arrangement across the paper over this line. Alternate the makes and lengths of the wrappers.

3 Carefully cut out each letter using a craft knife and scissors.

**Sticking down the letters**
4 Use PVA adhesive to stick the letters across the file in a haphazard arrangement. Repeat to stick letters across the notebook.

Stencil letters over the wrappers, using large ones for the file, small for the notebook.

**Fixing**
5 Give the file and notebook a good coat of spray fixative.

Mark a straight line across the paper, then stick sweet paper wrappers diagonally over it.

2 Mark out stencil letters over the stuck down wrappers. Use large letters for the file and small sized letters for the notebook.

**Monograms**
Choose initials of names to personalize school files, or use smaller letters and write the name in full. Boys might like their favourite football team emblazoned on their school files, and girls, the latest film or pop star.

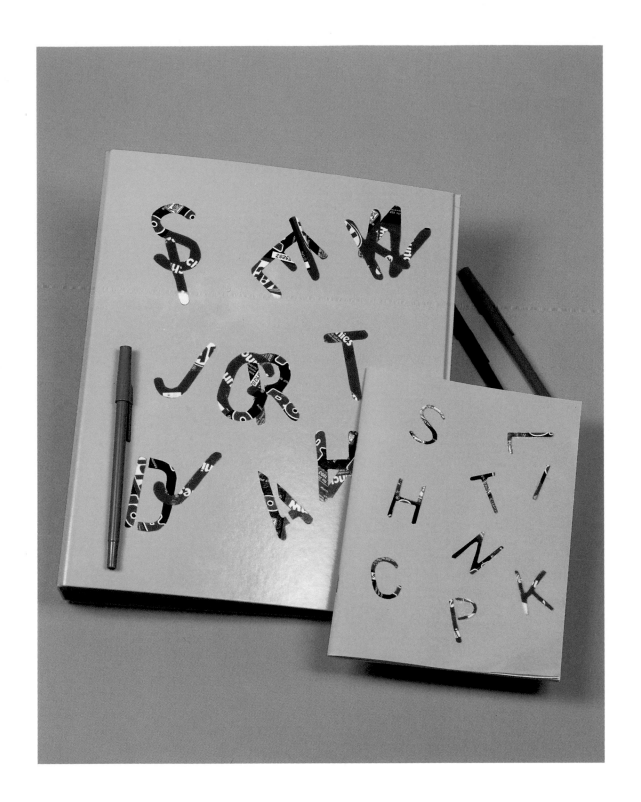

# Easter eggs and egg cups

*Bring Easter and a touch of spring to your breakfast table with decorated eggs – real or wooden – and matching egg cups all covered in Easter bunnies!*

**Materials**
Real eggs
White spray paint
Yellow and white matt craft paint
Small natural sponges
Self-adhesive stickers of bunnies and tiny
  flowers
Clear gloss varnish
Wooden egg cups

**Blowing the eggs**
1  First blow the eggs. Put each egg in an egg cup, hold a large darning needle over the end of the egg and gently tap with a hammer to pierce the shell.

2  Turn the egg over and make another hole in the opposite end. Very gently enlarge the hole in the narrow end of the egg using the needle.

3  Holding the egg over a bowl, blow through the smaller hole until the contents of the egg are forced out of the larger hole. Reserve the egg contents for cooking.

4  Wash out the egg shells and leave in a warm place to dry well before you start to decorate them (see page 68).

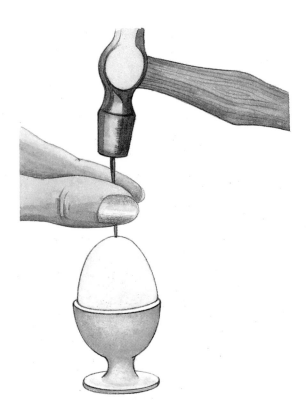

Gently tap the darning needle with a hammer to pierce the shell.

**Different eggs**
Although chicken's eggs are fine, for a 'larger than life' effect, use ducks' or goose eggs.
   If you prefer not to use real eggs, wooden eggs can be purchased from craft shops and then they can be decorated in a similar way.

## Eggs in a nest
If you prefer to decorate the eggs alone, and not the egg cups, display the découpaged eggs in a little 'nest' made out of twigs, moss, wild grasses and straw stuck to the inside and outside of an empty yogurt or margarine pot or a small plastic bowl – never take a bird's nest from the wild, since many species return, year after year, to the same nest.

Alternatively, display the eggs in a pretty wicker, moss or lavender basket, on a bed of fresh moss, straw or crumpled green tissue paper.

# Greetings cards

*Whatever the greeting – birthday, anniversary, a special thank you – a hand-made card will show you really care, especially when the motif has a raised 3-D effect.*

**Materials**
Card mounts
Masking tape and rough paper
Matt paint
Giftwrap paper with distinctive motifs
Spray adhesive
White typing paper
Small self-adhesive stickers
Spray fixative

**Painting the card**
**1** Spread open the 3 sections of the card mount. Tape a sheet of rough paper over the 2 outside sections, leaving the front section exposed. Dab a toothbrush in the paint. Hold the brush near the card front and brush over with a finger to spatter the paint over the card front. Leave to dry, then remove masking paper.

**Arranging the decoration**
**2** Choose the main motif for the card, then cut a piece of giftwrap paper to fit behind the card front so the main motif will be centred behind the opening. Using spray adhesive, fix the paper to the card section behind the opening.

**3** Fold the front of the card over and stick down to form the card.

**Creating the 3-D effect**
**4** From the giftwrap paper, roughly cut out the central motif three more times. Using spray adhesive, mount the motifs on to plain white paper. Carefully cut out each motif, following the same outline.

**5** Place a self-adhesive sticker in the centre of the central motif on the card. Stick one of the cut-out motifs exactly over the first one. Repeat, twice more until all the motifs are mounted one on top of the other.

**6** Give the card a coat of spray fixative.

Stick a cut-out motif exactly over the first one and repeat twice more.

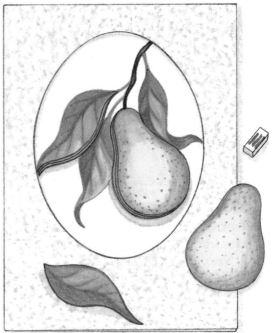

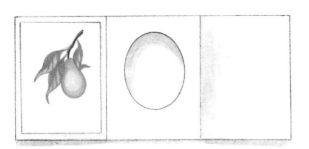

Using spray adhesive, fix the centred motif to the card section behind the opening.

# Gift wraps

*Cheer up plain brown paper or small carrier bags with clever cut-out shapes and flowers to make the perfect gift wrapping, and make your presents look too good to open!*

## Materials
Spray adhesive
Doileys
Plain carrier bag
Masking tape
Spray paint
Floral giftwrap paper
PVA adhesive
Spray fixative
Brightly-coloured ready-cut paper shapes
Plain brown wrapping paper
Water-based paints in co-ordinating
   colours

## Painting the carrier bag
**1** Spray adhesive over the wrong side of a doiley. Press the doiley over one side of the carrier bag and mask out the surrounding areas of the bag.

**2** Spray over the doiley with paint. Leave to dry, then carefully remove the doiley. Repeat on the other side of the bag.

**3** Carefully cut out flowers from the floral giftwrap. Using PVA adhesive, stick them in position over the painted motif.

**4** Spray over the whole bag with fixative.

### Cut-out shapes on paper
**1** Remove the cut-out shapes from their backing and stick them on to the brown paper in a random arrangement.

### Floral shapes on paper
**2** Carefully cut out flowers from the giftwrap paper. Using spray adhesive, stick the flowers at random over the brown paper.

**3** Pour a little of the paint into a saucer. Dip in a toothbrush. Hold the brush over the paper and rub over the brush head with a finger or small piece of card, to splatter the paint over the paper. Fade out the colour over the background.

**4** Spray over the decorated papers with fixative.

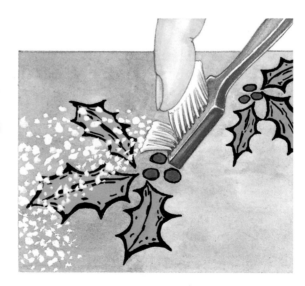

Spray over the doiley with paint, then leave to dry and remove the doiley.

Using a finger or small card, rub over the toothbrush to splatter paint over the paper.

---

### Christmas bags
At Christmas time decorate carrier bags with holly and berries.

# Christmas balls

*Hang a few brightly-coloured balls on the tree this Christmas, each one decorated with cheery Christmas motifs, cut from sheets of giftwrap paper.*

**Materials**
Cotton balls, 2in (5cm) in diameter
Red, green and mauve matt craft paint
Christmas giftwrap paper with small
 motifs
PVA adhesive
Glitter glue pens
Clear gloss varnish
Gold, red and green cord and small
 coloured wooden beads for hanging
Clear adhesive

**Painting the balls**
1 Paint the cotton balls in different colours and leave to dry.

**Adding the motifs**
2 Carefully cut out the motifs from the giftwrap paper. Divide up the motifs so there are different ones on each ball.

3 Dilute the PVA with a little water, then use it to stick the motifs round each ball. Carefully smooth the motifs round the ball, eliminating any air bubbles. Leave to dry.

Use glitter pens to decorate the motifs, then leave to dry thoroughly.

## Finishing

**4** Use the glitter glue pens to decorate the motifs. Leave to dry.

**5** Give each ball several coats of varnish, leaving them to dry between each coat.

## Threading on to cords

**6** Using a long needle, thread 16in (40cm) of cord through the centre of each ball. Thread through a bead and form a loop. Knot the cord above the bead. At the base, thread on a second bead and knot cord ends together to hold. Seal knot with a blob of clear adhesive.

> **Tip**
> Hold the balls on cocktail sticks held in Plasticine or florists' foam block while painting and varnishing.

**5** To cover the base, stand the covered ring on the wrong side of another piece of shiny red paper and mark round the outer and inner edges. Cut out ⅛in (3mm) inside the marked lines. Stick to the wrong side of card ring, covering the raw edges.

**Decorating the wreath**
**6** Roughly cut out bunches of holly leaves and berries from the giftwrap paper, making sure that you have 3 copies of each group.

Cut out sprigs of holly leaves and berries, making sure that you have 3 of each group.

**7** Using spray adhesive, stick the holly groups on to white paper. Carefully cut out using manicure scissors.

**8** Arrange 1 set of each group round the shiny red ring. When the arrangement looks right, fix the arrangement in place by sticking each group to the ring with a self-adhesive sticker placed in the centre of the back of the holly group.

Stick a third group of holly leaves round the wreath exactly over the previous set.

**9** Stick the second set of holly groups round the ring exactly matching the edges of the previous groups, but placing 2 self-adhesive stickers behind each group.

**10** Stick the third group of holly leaves round the wreath over the previous set, exactly matching the outer edges and using 2 self-adhesive stickers between the 2 layers.

**The right spot**
Although this wreath, even with its 2 coats of fixative, is too delicate to be fully exposed to the weather, it would look lovely on the front door inside a covered or open porch. Inside, hang it above a mantelpiece, or make two wreaths and hang them either side of a fireplace, sofa or Christmas tree.

**Finishing**

**11** Give the whole wreath 2 coats of gloss spray fixative, allowing it to dry between the coats.

**12** Fasten a small plate hanger to the back of the wreath for hanging.

Fasten a small plate hanger to the back of the wreath for hanging.

As well as holly leaves, Christmas wreaths can be made in the same way using flowers or Christmas fruits. However, as you need at least 3 layers of each motif, you may need to buy several sheets of similar wrapping paper.

The self-adhesive stickers can be layered in different proportions to give various heights to the arrangement.

Why not use flower and foliage books for reference. Look at various natural wreaths, find similar flowers and leaves in paper and reproduce these arrangements.

The basic wreath can also be lightly padded to give it a rounded appearance. Insert a thin layer of foam rubber between the covering paper and the card ring. Cut the foam slightly smaller than the card ring, carefully smooth the paper over the edge and stick to the back in the usual way.

# Noah's ark

*Let it rain – old Noah and his family, and the animals, will be safe from the deluge in this smart ark. The one pictured measures approximately 22in (56cm) long by 10in (25cm) wide.*

**Materials**
Sheet of flexible card
Square or rectangular box for the cabin
Corrugated card
Adhesive tape
Masking tape
Clear, quick-drying glue
PVA adhesive

Brown parcel paper
White emulsion paint
Brown wax crayon
Acrylic paints

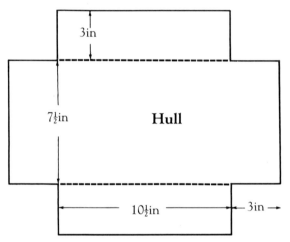

Draw the main hull on cardboard.

Cut the cardboard box for the cabin.

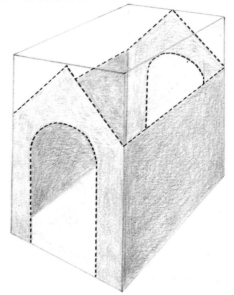

70

## Preparation

**1** Draw the main hull shape on cardboard. Score along the dotted lines and fold.

**2** Cut the cardboard box to shape so that it has gable ends and a doorway.

**3** Cut 2 ark sides from doubled corrugated cardboard.

**4** Tape the ark sides to the hull, then bend up the ends of the deck to fit inside the hull.

Cut 2 ark sides from doubled corrugated card.

**5** Tape across the underside of the prow and stern.

**6** Glue the cabin inside the hull.

**7** Cover the entire ark inside and out with pasted strips of newspaper. Leave to dry.

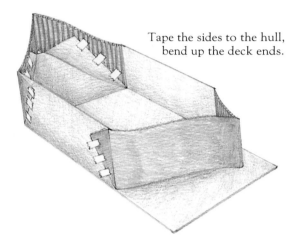

Tape the sides to the hull, bend up the deck ends.

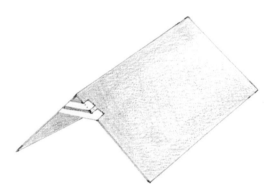

Tape across the roof ends to hold the shape.

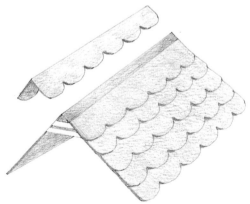

Cut scallops on one edge of the card strips.
Cut scallops on both edges of the roof ridge.
Stick the tiles to the roof, overlapping each strip.

**8** Apply 3 more layers. Gently pull the sides of the ark outwards to a bow shape while the papier mâché is still damp.

**9** When the hull has been shaped and the work is dry, apply 2 more layers of newspaper strips.

**Roof**

**10** Cut a piece of card and score it down the middle so that it fits the cabin roof. Fold the roof and then tape across the ends to hold the shape.

**11** From thick card, cut 10 strips to the length of the roof and 1½in (4cm) deep. Cut the ridge to the same width and twice the depth. Score down the middle of the ridge and fold.

**12** Mark and cut scallops along one edge of the strips and on both edges of the ridge piece.

**13** Starting at the lower edge of the roof, glue scalloped tiles to the roof sides, overlapping each strip a little. Finally, glue the ridge piece in position.

**14** Cover the underside of the roof with 2–3 layers of pasted newspaper strips. Leave to dry.

**15** Cover the top side of the roof with 3 layers of pasted tissue paper, pressing the tissue down between the scallops. Leave to dry. The roof remains free of the cabin so that the animals can be put in and taken out easily.

**Finishing**

**16** Tear long strips of brown paper and glue inside the hull for the deck. Mark the plank lines with wax crayon.

**17** Paint the ark as in the picture, or in colours of your choice. The window effect on the cabin wall can be painted on or you can cut rectangles of plain, coloured paper and paste them in a window arrangement.

# Mr and Mrs Noah and the animals

*The basic animal shapes given can be adapted to all kinds of animals. The smaller structure will make dogs and sheep. The larger structure could be adapted to make lions, tigers, zebras etc.*

## Materials
Plastic coated wire
Kitchen paper roll
Wallpaper paste, mixed thickly
Small pieces of cardboard
PVA adhesive
White emulsion paint
Acrylic paints

## Preparation
**1** Working from the outlines, bend and twist wire into animal and human shapes. It does not matter how large you make the figures as long as they fit into your ark. The human figure stands 9in (22.5cm) tall, while the zebra is 8in long and 6in tall (20 × 15cm).

## Working the design
**2** Tear long strips of kitchen paper and spread paste on one side. Wrap the wire structures with pasted strips, leave to dry.

**3** Apply a second layer, building up the thicker places – heads, bodies etc. Add more strips as desired until you are satisfied with the shape.

**4** Leave the animals and figures to dry then paint with PVA adhesive.

**5** Cut ears and tails from card. Stick to the animals.

**6** Paint the animals and figures with white emulsion paint.

**7** Decorate the animals with acrylic paints.

## Dressing the figures
**8** Wrap the figures in kitchen paper and stick the overlaps to fasten. Paint the clothes (see picture) then the faces.

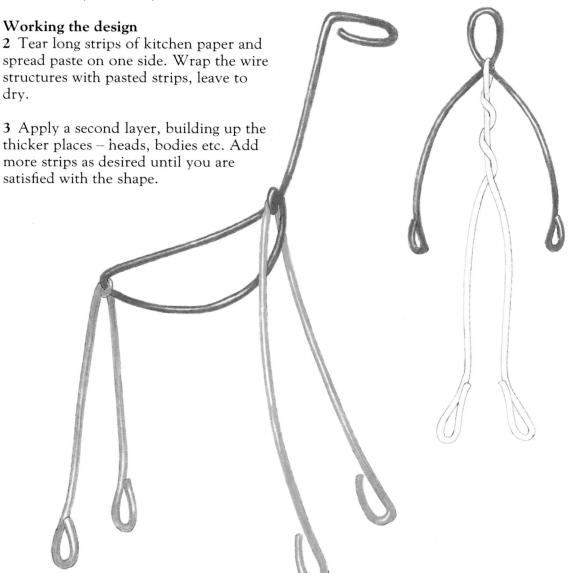

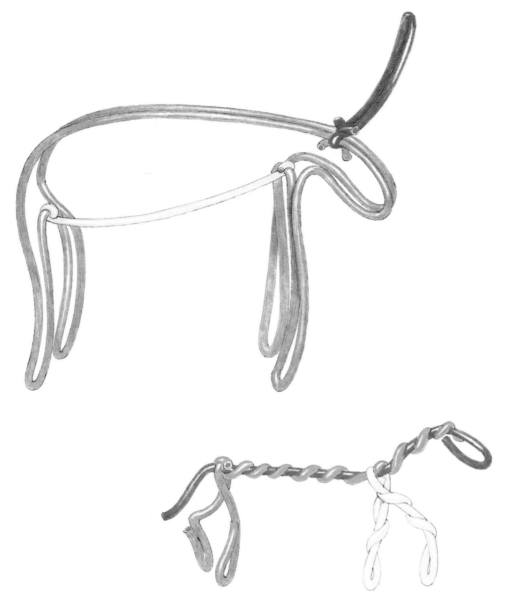

Bend wire to make the human and animals shapes.
Wrap the wire structure with pasted strips,
building up the head and body.

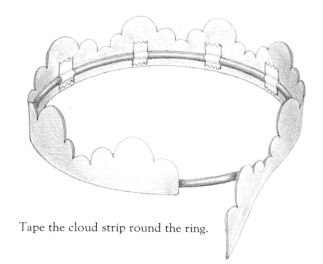

Tape the cloud strip round the ring.

# Sheep mobile

*Hang this amusing mobile in the bedroom and the children can literally count sheep. The effect of the sheep's woolly coats is made with paper pulp applied over card shapes.*

## Materials
Cardboard
3–4 cups of paper pulp (refer to Better Techniques)
6 large jump rings
Acrylic paints
Wire lampshade ring, approximately 8in (20cm) diameter
Masking tape
Tissue paper
PVA adhesive
Nylon thread; brass curtain ring

## Preparation
1 Trace the sheep shape. Cut 8 sheep from card.

## Working the design
2 Smear paper pulp over the sheep, leaving the face area and feet. Leave to dry then turn over and do the other side of the sheep.

3 Build up the body thickness with 2 more layers of pulp, leaving each to dry between applications. Work both sides of the sheep in the same way, but always leaving the face and feet untreated.

4 Pierce a hole in the back of the sheep. Slip a jump ring through.

5 Paint the sheep fleece white and the feet and face black. Paint in the eyes.

6 Cover the wire ring with masking tape.

7 Wrap the ring with pasted tissue until the wire is thickened and smooth.

8 Trace the cloud pattern. Measure the circumference of the ring and cut a 1in (2.5cm) wide strip of card to the measurement plus 1in (2.5cm) for overlap.

9 Trace the cloud motif along the strip. Cut out.

10 Tape the cloud strip to the outside of the ring then paste tissue over the join. Cover the cloud strip with pasted tissue. Apply 2–3 layers.

11 Pierce 8 equidistant holes round the cloud edge.

12 Cut 4 lengths of thread. Tape one end to the inside of the cloud, spacing the 4 threads equidistantly. Knot the 4 ends and tie to a curtain ring.

13 Hang the clouds ring so that you can work on it. Pass threads through the 8 holes and knot. Thread the other end through the sheep's jump rings and knot.

14 Hang the sheep at alternate heights, one high, one low.

Trace the sheep shape.
Cut 6 from card.

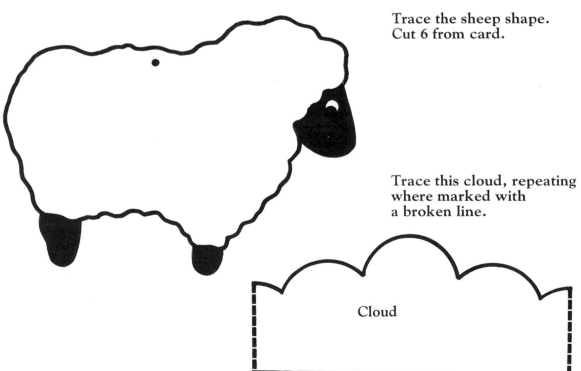

Trace this cloud, repeating
where marked with
a broken line.

Cloud

# Fairy doll

*This little toy is almost literally made from nothing at all – just icecream sticks, a cardboard tube and a pingpong ball – plus some clever papier mâché.*

**Materials**
Cardboard tube, 3½in (8cm) long and 2in (5cm) in diameter
4 wooden icecream sticks (or flat pieces of wood, 4½ × ½in (11 × 1cm)
4 small beads; silver wire
White emulsion paint
PVA adhesive; tissue paper; acrylic paints
Knitting yarns; small bead
White satin fabric
White net
Cocktail stick
Paper star

**Preparation**
**1** Pierce holes at each side of the cardboard tube ⅛in (3mm) from the top edge for the arm fixtures.

**2** Pierce holes to align ⅛in (3mm) from the bottom edge for fixing the legs.

**3** Cut two of the sticks in half for the arms.

**4** Pierce holes at the cut ends of both arm pieces.

**5** Pierce holes at one end of the remaining sticks for legs.

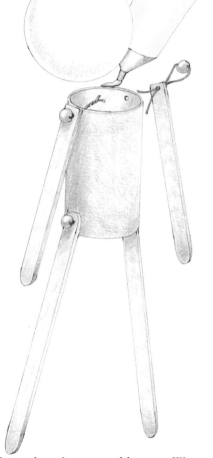

Pierce holes at the sides, top and bottom. Wire on the limbs, stick on the head.

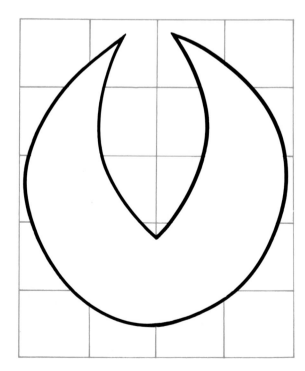

Draw this wing pattern on squared paper, scale 1 sq = 1in (2.5cm).

78

**6 Assembly:** Cut four 2in (5cm) lengths of wire. Slip a bead on a wire, pass the end through a limb then through a hole in the tube. Twist the wire ends. Work all four limbs in the same way.

**7** Glue the ball head on the top of the tube using quick-drying glue.

**8** Draw the wings shape and cut from thin card. Stick the wings to the back of the tube body and paint silver.

**9** Wrap the arms and legs with long, pasted strips of tissue paper. When dry, apply a second layer.

**10** Cover the doll's body, head and neck with pasted scraps of tissue paper. Leave to dry then apply 2 more layers.

**11** Paint the entire doll with emulsion paint.

**12** Paint the doll's features. Cut lengths of mixed yarns and glue across the head.

**13** Cut a 12in (30cm) square each of white satin and net. Fold the squares, wrong sides facing. Gather and sew the satin round the doll's waist. Gather and sew the net skirt on top. Cut a net strip and tie round the waist. Make a net bow and stick to the forehead. Stick on a bead.

**14** Paint the cocktail stick, fix the paper star to the end and stick the wand to the doll's hand.

# Punch and Judy

*These puppets have been favourites with generations of children. Although today's children are sometimes more sophisticated, the magic of a Punch and Judy show is as strong as ever.*

## Materials
Newspaper
Garden sticks, dowel rods etc, approximately 8in (20cm) long (one for each puppet)
Paper pulp mixed with PVA adhesive ($\frac{2}{3}$ pulp to $\frac{1}{3}$ adhesive) (refer to Better Techniques for making pulp)
Mixed wallpaper paste
Tissue paper
Cardboard
Acrylic paints
18in (45cm) gathered lace edging
$\frac{1}{4}$in (6mm)-wide red satin ribbon
6in (15cm) of $\frac{1}{4}$in (6mm)-wide white satin ribbon
12in (30cm) of $\frac{1}{4}$in (6mm)-wide white satin ribbon
3 bells
Blue fabric, 24in (60cm) square
Wide-striped cotton fabric 24in (60cm) square
Narrow-striped fabric, 12 × 4in (30 × 10cm)
White fabric 12 × 4in (30 × 10cm)
36in (90cm) of navy ricrac braid
White cotton fabric, 12in (30cm) square
Flat icecream stick

## Preparation
**1** Crumple newspaper into an oval shape, about 4in (10cm) by 3in (7.5cm) across for the head. Push a stick into the underside of the head. Tape the head to hold the shape. Tape round the bottom of the head and on to the stick to make a neck. Tape down the stick. Make two heads in the same way for Punch and Judy.

**2** Trace hand shapes for both puppets. Cut from card.

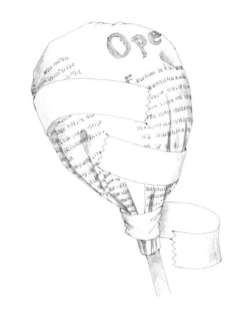

Tape the newspaper head to the stick.

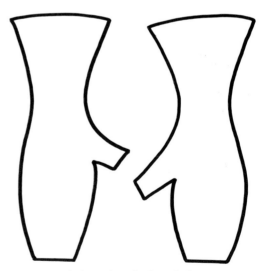

**Trace left and right hand shapes.**

## Working the design
**3** Stand the stick in a container that will hold the head steady while you model the features.

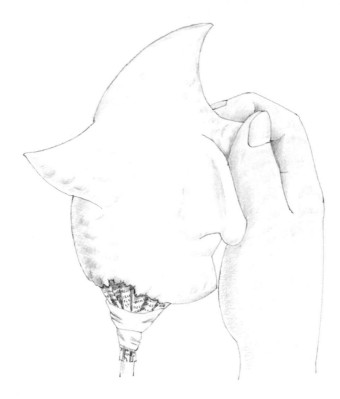

Mould pulp on to the head to get the basic features.

**5** When the faces are modelled, apply 3 layers of pasted tissue over the faces and down the sticks.

**6** Trace the pattern and cut Judy's scalloped cap front from card. Cover the cap front with pasted tissue on both sides. Leave to dry and apply 2 more layers. Paint the cap front white.

**7** Glue the cap front round Judy's head.

**8 Faces and hands:** Paint the puppets' heads pale pink. **Punch:** Paint a black outline round the face for the cap edge and paint the three-pointed cap black. Paint a red mask and a red mouth. Paint white eye patches with black crosses for the eyes. **Judy:** Paint black dots for eyes. Paint dark pink cheeks. Brush in brown eyebrows and a curl on the forehead. Give Judy a wide, red, smile.

**9** Brush a coat of diluted PVA over both puppet heads. Build up one side of the hands with pulp. Leave to dry then cover the hands with pasted tissue. Leave to dry then apply another layer of tissue. Paint the hands pink.

**Trace this brim for Judy's cap.**

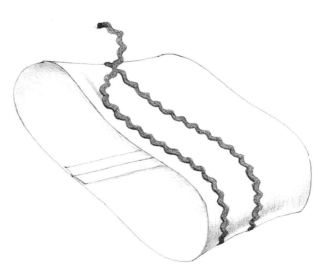

Join the ruffle ends and stick ricrac braid round the middle and near the edge.

**4** Using your fingers, mould pulp on to the heads to get the basic shape of the puppets' features. Punch has a large nose and chin and a three-pointed cap on his head. Judy has a neater, pointed nose and chin. Do not work too quickly. Do the modelling over several sessions, leaving each application of pulp to dry out thoroughly.

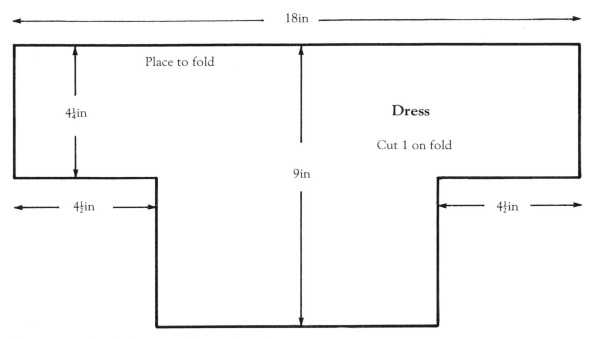

18in

Place to fold

$4\frac{1}{4}$in

**Dress**

Cut 1 on fold

9in

$4\frac{1}{2}$in

$4\frac{1}{2}$in

Draw a pattern for both puppets' dresses from this diagram.

**Dressing the puppets**
**10 Judy:** Stick gathered lace edging round the head, behind the cap front. Tie a small red ribbon bow and stick to the top of the head.

**11** From the diagram, cut Judy's dress in the wide-striped fabric. Snip a neck hole.

**12** Neaten the sleeve ends. Stitch the side and underarm seams in one.

**13** Turn and stitch the hem. Turn a narrow hem on the sleeve ends. Slip in the hands and gather the sleeves tightly to hold the hands.

**14** Slip the dress on to the puppet stick. Stick the neckline to the stick.

**15 Ruffle:** Join the short ends of the ruffle fabric. Stick the ricrac braid round, just above the middle and $1\frac{1}{4}$in (3cm) away.

**16** Fold the ruffle along the middle wrong sides facing and gather both raw edges together. Slip over the puppet's head and pull up the gathers tightly. Knot the thread ends to secure.

**17 Punch:** Make a dark blue garment in the same way as Judy's dress. Insert the hands as for Judy.

**18** Make a ruffle as for Judy's but without the ricrac braid decoration. Slip on to the puppet.

**19** Pierce the points of Punch's cap. Thread fine wire through and slip on the bells.

### Punch's stick

**20** Tear small pieces of kitchen roll paper and paste round an icecream stick, so that it is thicker at one end. Finish with 2 layers of pasted tissue.

**21** When dry, paint the stick white. Tie a red ribbon bow round the base of the stick. Stick to Punch's hand with PVA adhesive.

# Judy's baby

### Materials
Tin foil
Newspaper
Mixed wallpaper paste
Tissue paper
Acrylic paints
Piece of white cotton fabric 8in (20cm) square
6in (15cm) piece of pre-gathered lace

### Preparation
**1** Crumple tin foil into a 1½in (3cm)-diameter ball. Crumple more tinfoil into a 3 × 1in (7.5 × 2.5cm) sausage shape.

### Working the design
**2** Tape the ball and sausage shape together. Tear newspaper into small strips and paste all over the figure. Leave to dry. Apply 2 more layers of pasted newspaper strips.

**3** Paste two layers of tissue paper over the ball head.

**4** Paint the face pink.

**5** Lay the baby figure on the square of white fabric. Wrap the baby and stick the fabric in place.

**6** Stick gathered lace edging round the face.

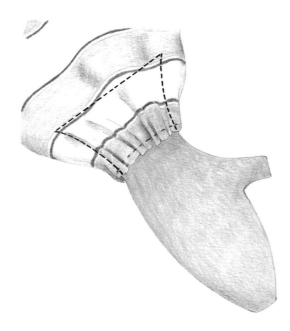

Gather the sleeves round the hand and pull up the gathers tightly.

Tape the ball and sausage shapes together.

# Mushroom savings bank

*What fun to have a money box that looks as though it came out of a fairy story! The mushroom makes a perfect gift for children – and perhaps it will encourage them to save.*

### Materials
A bowl, about 7in (18cm) diameter
Petroleum jelly
2 cups of mixed paper pulp (refer to
  Better Techniques)
Cardboard tube, about 3in (7.5cm)
  diameter, 4in (10cm) long
Thin cardboard
Kitchen paper roll
Tissue paper
Mixed wallpaper paste
Adhesive tape
Masking tape
White emulsion paint
Acrylic paints
PVA adhesive

### Preparation
1  Grease the inside of the bowl.

### Working the design
2  Spread pulp on the bottom of the bowl and about halfway up the sides. Try and keep the top edge even. Leave to dry.

3  When dry, fill in any cracks with more pulp. Even up the edges with pulp. Leave to dry again then remove the shell from the mould carefully.

### Working the design
4  Cut a circle of card to fit the bottom of the tube. Tape in place

5  Take 3 sheets of kitchen paper, fold in four then tape round the sealed end of the tube.

6  Cover the tube and base with a layer of pasted tissue paper. Leave until dry. Apply 2 more layers, leaving the work to dry between each application.

7  Using a sharp crafts knife, cut a money slit across the middle of the mushroom cap.

8  Measure the depth of the mushroom cap. Cut a strip of card to this depth by the circumference of the tube plus ½in (1cm). Overlap the strip ends and tape to form a collar.

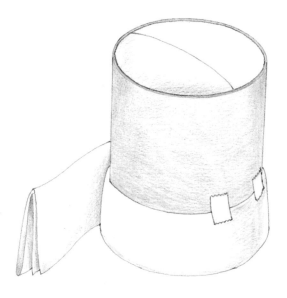

Tape folded kitchen paper round the bottom of the tube to thicken the base.

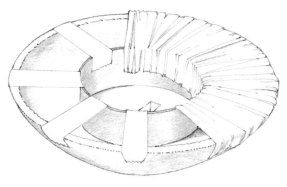

Hold the inside collar in place with masking tape strips, cover with creased, pasted tissue paper.

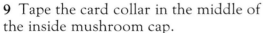

**9** Tape the card collar in the middle of the inside mushroom cap.

**10** Using masking tape, fix strips from the inside of the collar to the outside of the mushroom cap.

**11** Cover the tapes with pasted strips of tissue paper. Crease the strips as you apply them so that they look like the gills of a mushroom.

**12** Paint the finished mushroom and cap with acrylic colours. Give a final coat of diluted PVA adhesive.

**Toad Hall**
To vary the design, paint a blue door and 2 windows on the mushroom stalk. Paint a bell pull on the right and some small flowers round the bottom of the mushroom.

# Sun mirror

*This magical-looking mirror is decorated with the sun, stars and clouds above and waves and starfish below. It is sure to have pride of place in your home.*

**Materials**
8in (20cm) square mirror
10in (25cm) square of hardboard
4 sticky pads
Corrugated cardboard
Brown paper tape
Thick stem wire, 8in (20cm) long
Clear, adhesive tape
PVA adhesive
12 cocktail sticks
Thin cardboard
Pulp cardboard fruit packing (refer to
    Better Techniques)
Mixed paper pulp (refer to Better
    Techniques)
Mixed wallpaper paste
Tissue paper
Clear, quick-drying adhesive
White emulsion paint
Gold paint
Bronze-coloured cream paint (Treasure
    gold)

**Preparation**
**1** Fasten the mirror to the hardboard with sticky pads.

**2** Cut 2 pieces of corrugated card 6 × 1½in (15 × 3cm).

**3** Fix them to the sides of the mirror with strips of brown paper tape.

**4** Bend the stem wire into a semi-circle. Tape it to the centre top of the hardboard.

**5** Moisten pieces of brown paper tape and cover the wire.

**6** Cut 2 strips from the pulp cardboard fruit packing. Stick one overlapping the other across the bottom of the mirror for waves. The strips should overlap the bottom edges of the side pillars.

**7** Cut pieces of card with scalloped 'cloud' edges. Stick the clouds round the top of the mirror, overlapping some on to the mirror edges. Cut another cloud-edged strip and stick it down the right-hand edge of the mirror, overlapping on to the glass.

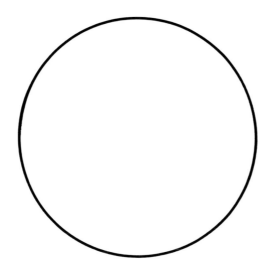

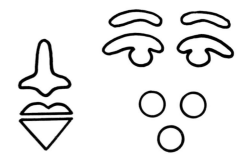

**Trace these shapes to decorate the mirror.**

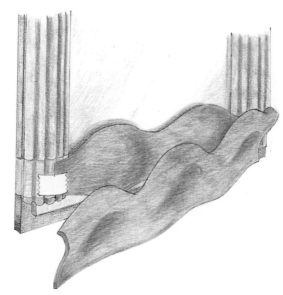

Cut strips from fruit packing. Stick strips overlapping for waves.

Overlap cloud shapes on to the mirror edges.

### Working the design

**8** Paste torn pieces of newspaper across the wired semi-circle. Apply more pasted pieces across the hardboard and mirror edges and across the straight edges of the cloud strips.

**9** Paste pieces of tissue across the clouds, the sun's semi-circle backing and the waves. When the first layer is dry, apply 2–3 more layers, allowing the pasted tissue to crumple as you work.

**10** Trace the patterns. From thin card, cut 2 pillar tops, 2 eyes and eyebrows for the sun, 2 cheeks, a nose and a chin. Cut 3 eight-pointed stars. Cut 2 five-pointed stars.

**11** Trace the 2 sun ray patterns. Cut 6 of each from thin card. Cut a $2\frac{1}{4}$in (6cm)-diameter circle of card for the sun's face.

**12** Glue the cocktail sticks to the wire across the semi-circle and on to the top of the mirror.

**13** Glue the sun rays on to the cocktail sticks, alternating the shapes.

**14** Build up the thickness of the sun rays with pulp. When dry, wrap the rays with pasted tissue.

**15** Stick the sun's face over the rays. Build up the surface with pulp. When dry, paste tissue over the edges of the circle.

### Finishing

**16** Stick the features on the sun's face. Stick the eight-point stars to the clouds. Stick the tops of the pillars in place. Stick the five-point star starfish below the waves. Paste tissue over everything.

**17** Paste tissue over the pillar tops and pillars.

**18** If there are spaces in your design that appear to need filling, paste pieces of pasted kitchen roll paper down for cloud effects.

**19** Paint the finished piece with white emulsion paint. When it is dry, paint gold. Finally, finger-dab over the gold with bronze.

**20** Apply 2–3 layers of pasted, torn newspaper strips to the back of the mirror. When the papier mâché is completely dry, paint the surface gold.

# Smiling sun

*Simply made on a cardboard base, this wall plaque looks solid and metallic when finished with a coat of gold paint. It makes an ideal decoration for a dark corner or a hallway.*

## Materials
Thick cardboard
Clear, quick-drying glue
Thin, flexible cardboard
Cocktail sticks
Mixed paper pulp (refer to Better
   Techniques)
Kitchen paper roll
Mixed wallpaper paste
Gold paint
Black paint

## Preparation
**1** Cut 2 circles of thick card, 6½in and
5½in diameter (16 and 13cm diameter).

**2** Using a large coin as a template, cut 10
circles of kitchen paper. Put aside.

**3** Mark the larger card circle into
quarters, then make 2 equidistant marks
in each quarter segment.

**4** Glue cocktail sticks at each mark so
that they protrude over the edge of the
card about three-quarters of their length.

**5** Trace the sun ray shapes. Transfer to
thin card and cut 6 of each shape.

**6** Alternating shapes, tape them to the
cocktail sticks.

**7** Glue the smaller card circle to cover
the ends of the cocktail sticks. Leave to
dry.

## Working the design
**8** Using 1 cup of mixed paper pulp,
spread a thin layer all over the sun. Leave
to dry. If cracks appear, fill them with
more pulp and leave to dry.

**9** Model the face with pulp and then
with small pieces of pasted newspaper.

**10** Build up the sun rays with pulp, then
with pasted newspaper strips.

**11** Paste 5 paper circles, one on another,
on each side of the sun's face for cheeks.

**12** When the work is completely dry,
paint the sun with 2 coats of white
emulsion paint.

**13** Paint the sun gold then, when dry,
rub black paint into the folds and
crevices using a scrap of fabric.

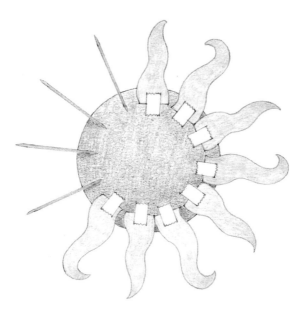

Alternating shapes, tape the rays to the cocktail
sticks.

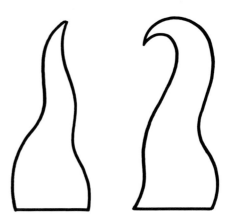

**Trace these sun rays.**

# Easter hen

*Make this colourful hen and bowl for your Easter breakfast table. Crumple a yellow paper serviette in the bowl and arrange the breakfast eggs in the 'nest'.*

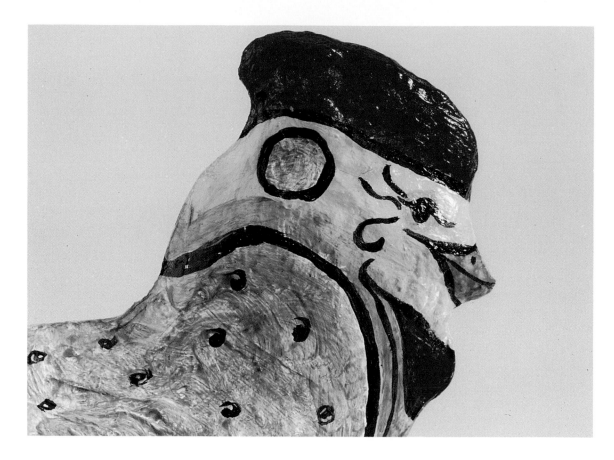

**Materials**
An inflated round balloon
Newspaper torn into small pieces
Tissue paper
Mixed wallpaper paste
PVA adhesive
Kitchen roll paper
Acrylic paints

**Preparation**
**1** Set the balloon in a cereal bowl to keep it steady while you work.

**Working the design**
**2** Dampen pieces of torn newspaper and apply to the surface of the balloon. Leave to dry, then apply pasted pieces of newspaper over the balloon.

**3** When dry, apply a second layer of pasted newspaper. Leave to dry then apply 4–5 more layers, leaving the work to dry between each layer.

**4** Pop the balloon and remove it from the paper shell. Trim the shell edges.

**5** Trace the head and tail patterns. Cut from card. Fix in place on the paper shell with pieces of sticky tape.

**6** Crumple little pads of tissue and tape them on either side of the head and tail to build them up.

**7** Paste small pieces of kitchen roll paper over the tissue pads to smooth out the surface.

**8** Paste 2 layers of tissue paper all over the hen to smooth off the surface.

**Bowl**
**9** Smear petroleum jelly round the inside of a bowl a little bigger than the circumference of the hen body.

**10** Cover the inside of the bowl with pasted newspaper strips. Leave to dry, then repeat the process 3–4 times. When completely dry, twist the paper shell and lift from the bowl.

**11** Trim the edge of the bowl into scallops.

**12** Cut a strip of card ¾in (18mm) deep by 20in (50cm). Tape the ends to make a circle. Tape the circle to the underside of the bowl for a standing rim.

**13** Paste tissue all over the outside of the bowl and over the edges of the standing rim. Leave to dry, then apply 2 more layers.

**14** Paste tissue to the inside of the bowl in the same way. Build up the inside of the bowl until the hen lid sits neatly in the bowl.

**15** Tear narrow strips of tissue and paste them over the scalloped edge.

**16** Paint the hen and bowl, inside and out, with white emulsion paint.

**17** Paint the bowl red with a black trim. Paint the hen, following the picture.

**18** Varnish the finished hen and bowl on the outside or coat with diluted PVA adhesive.

Tape the head to the body, tape crumpled tissue each side of the head.

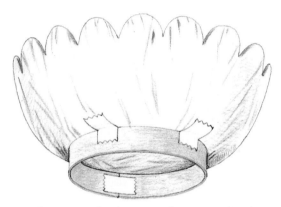

Tape the strip ends, then tape the ring under the bowl for a rim.

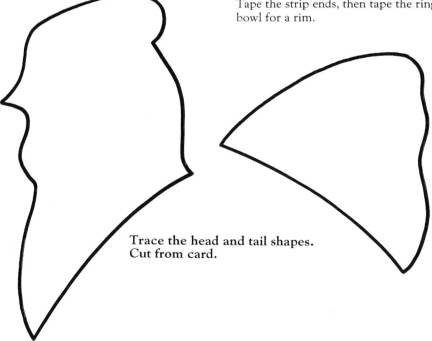

**Trace the head and tail shapes. Cut from card.**

# Egg-cups

*Children will love making their own breakfast egg-cups from egg trays and they can decorate them in any way they like. Why not make one for each member of the family for Easter?*

## Materials
Pulp paper egg tray
PVA adhesive
Clear, sticky tape
Tissue paper
Flour and water paste (refer to Better
   Techniques)
White emulsion paint
Acrylic paints
Clear, polyurethane varnish

## Preparation
1 Cut sections from the egg tray as large as possible. There will be gaps where the sections adjoin. These are filled with tape later.

2 Cut more sections and trim these down to approximately ⅝in (15mm) deep. These are for the egg-cup bases.

3 Stick the egg-cups to bases. If there are gaps in the edges of the cup or base, tape across the gaps.

Tape over any gaps in the sections. Stick the egg-cup to the base piece.

## Candle holders
Egg carton segments make pretty candle holders for party tables. Stick trimmed segments to squares of thick card. Cut 4 petals from carton pieces, tape to the cup edges. Paste over 5–6 layers of tissue. Paint and varnish.

## Working the design
4 Cover the entire egg-cup with pieces of pasted tissue. Leave to dry out then repeat the process 6 more times, leaving each layer to dry before applying the next.

5 When dry, paint the egg-cups with white emulsion paint. Decorate with acrylic colours. Varnish inside and out.

## Decorating egg-cups
Painted egg-cups make acceptable gifts and can be presented at Easter, complete with a fresh egg or a chocolate egg. If you cannot draw, decorate egg-cups with stencilled designs – there are many small, suitable stencil motifs to be found in crafts shops. Alternatively, cut motifs from coloured magazine pages and paste them to the egg-cup. Varnish over the decoration several times until the edges of the cut-outs can no longer be felt with a finger nail. Rub-down letters can also be used to make initials or words.

# Rose bowl

*The paper pulp method is used to make this bowl and the secret of success lies in ensuring that the pulp is applied inside the bowl evenly and smoothly.*

Bowl for a mould
Petroleum jelly
4 cups of mixed paper pulp (refer to
    Better Techniques)
Fine sandpaper
Acrylic paints
PVA adhesive
Clear polyurethane varnish

**Preparation**
1  Grease the inside of the bowl with petroleum jelly.

**Working the design**
2  Press an even layer of pulp, $\frac{1}{4}$in (6mm) thick, to the inside of the bowl. Begin at the bottom of the bowl and work up the sides. Leave to dry.

3  If cracks appear after drying, fill them with more pulp and smooth out the surface. Leave to dry again.

Press an even layer of pulp inside the bowl.

**4** Twist the pulp bowl gently to remove it from the mould.

**5** If there are uneven places on the edges, fill out with paper pulp. Leave to dry.

**6** Rub the edges of the bowl with sandpaper for a smooth finish.

**7** Paint the bowl inside and out in a plain colour or in a decorative pattern, such as the simple rose design in the picture.

**8** Give the finished bowl 2 coats of diluted PVA adhesive or 4–5 coats of polyurethane varnish. Leave each coat to dry before applying the next.

# Scalloped bowl

*In this project, the bowl is shaped over a round balloon which is popped after the papier mâché has dried. The edges of the bowl are then cut into scallops but they can be left straight if you prefer.*

**Materials**
Round balloon, inflated
Newspaper torn into small pieces
Tissue paper
Kitchen paper roll
Wallpaper paste, mixed thickly
PVA adhesive
Giftwrap paper
Gold modeller's paint

**Preparation**
1 Place the inflated balloon in a suitable container to support it while you work.

**Working the design**
2 Paste small pieces of newspaper and apply them to the surface of the ballon, overlapping the edges slightly. Cover just over half of the balloon's surface.

3 When the first layer is dry, apply another layer and leave to dry.

4 Apply 3 more layers in the same way.

5 Prick the balloon to deflate it and gently pull it away from the papier mâché.

6 Use a small lid to mark scallops round the edge of the bowl. Cut with sharp scissors.

7 Using newspaper and kitchen paper alternately, paste layers of strips over the inside and outside of the bowl until a thickness has been built up. Take care that you keep the shape of the scalloped edges. You will find that narrow strips of paper work best here. Leave the work to dry out between each layer.

Mark scallops round the bowl.

Use narrow strips of paper over the scalloped edge.

**8** Apply a final layer of pasted tissue to give a smooth finish, inside and out.

### Decorating the bowl

**9** Tear pieces of giftwrap and paste over the outside of the bowl, overlapping pieces for an attractive effect. Alternatively, if the giftwrap design is suitable, cut motifs from the paper and apply these to the bowl, overlapping them so that the surface is covered.

**10** When the bowl is dry, brush on a coat of diluted PVA adhesive inside and out. Leave to dry.

**11** Paint the scalloped edge with gold paint.

**12** If you prefer, coat the bowl with white emulsion paint then decorate with a painted design.

# Bowl of cherries

*Display lots of these luscious-looking cherries in a papier mâché bowl for a pretty ornament. The bowl can be made with either the paper pulp or layered paper methods.*

**Materials**
Black (annealed) stem wires
Mixed paper pulp (refer to Better
  Techniques)
White paper
Acrylic paints
PVA adhesive

**Preparation**
1 Cut the stem wire to 2½in (6cm) long for double cherry stems and to 1¼in (3cm) for single cherries. Bend the longer wires in half.

**Working the design**
2 Mould small cherry-sized balls and press them on to the wire ends. Leave to dry, filling any cracks as they appear.

3 **Leaves:** Cut rectangles of paper, 1½ × ¾in (4 × 2cm). Paste 2 rectangles of paper together with a stem wire between, leaving a long end protruding. Leave to dry, then paint green on both sides.

4 Give the leaves a coat of diluted PVA adhesive on the top side only and leave to dry.

5 Cut the leaves to shape.

Mould cherry-sized balls from pulp and press on to the wire ends.

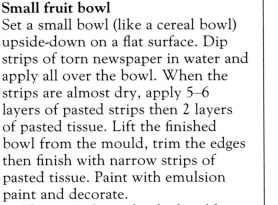

Paste wire between 2 paper rectangles. Paint the paper green, cut out leaf shapes.

---

**Small fruit bowl**
Set a small bowl (like a cereal bowl) upside-down on a flat surface. Dip strips of torn newspaper in water and apply all over the bowl. When the strips are almost dry, apply 5–6 layers of pasted strips then 2 layers of pasted tissue. Lift the finished bowl from the mould, trim the edges then finish with narrow strips of pasted tissue. Paint with emulsion paint and decorate.

Alternatively, make the bowl by greasing the inside with petroleum jelly and press paper pulp to the bottom and sides.

**6** Paint the cherries and the stems. Give the cherries only a coat of diluted PVA adhesive for a glossy finish.

**7** Fix the leaves to the fruit stems by twisting the wires together. Bend the leaf tips for a natural effect.

# Tea tray

*Creating this smart papier mâché tea tray could not be easier. All you need is an inexpensive plastic tray for a mould plus pasted newspaper – and some decorative giftwrap.*

## Materials
Metal or plastic tray
Petroleum jelly
Newspaper torn into small strips
Mixed wallpaper paste
Kitchen roll paper
Patterned giftwrap
PVA adhesive
Clear polyurethane varnish

## Preparation
1  Smear petroleum jelly over the surface of the tray.

## Working the design
2  Beginning at one side of the tray and working round the edges and towards the centre, paste newspaper strips to the tray. Overlap the pieces.

3  Leave the work to dry, then repeat the process 5–6 times, leaving the work to dry completely between each application.

4  Ease the paper shell from the tray.

5  Tear pieces of kitchen roll paper, paste them and apply a layer over the surface of the paper shell, over the edges and on to the back. Leave to dry.

6  Apply another layer to back and front but using newspaper strips this time.

7  Now work on the front of the tray only, applying alternate layers of newspaper and kitchen roll paper, leaving each layer to dry before working the next. Work 6–8 layers.

8  The tray should now be strong and inflexible. Add more layers if you think the tray requires strengthening.

9  When the last layer is dry, tear small pieces of giftwrap and paste them to the tray to cover the surface. When the paper is dry, other decorative motifs can be added. When the decoration is completed, brush diluted PVA over the tray.

10  Paint the back of the tray black. Give the front a final coat of polyurethane varnish.

At the end of the 18th century, Henry Clay of Birmingham, England, invented a way of making papier mâché by pasting whole sheets of paper together over a wood or metal core. Try the technique yourself to make a tray. Choose a square or rectangular metal or plastic tray. Work on a flat surface protected with plastic sheeting. Brush a large sheet of newspaper with wallpaper paste then carefully spread another sheet on top. Brush the surface with paste and place another sheet of newspaper on top. Try not to get creases in the paper. Work 12–15 layers. Leave the pasted paper to dry until it feels like a piece of leather. Grease the tray's surface. Lift the papier mâché on to the tray and press it to the tray's shape. Trim excess paper from the edges at this stage. Leave to dry slowly in a warm place. Finish the tray's edges with small strips of newspaper. Paint with emulsion and decorate.

# Seashore frame

*Here's a way to make good use of shells collected while on holiday. The basic idea could be adapted for a large, kitchen pinboard, or for a box top. Small pearl beads could be added for contrast.*

**Materials**
Frame cut from hardboard
Smaller ready-made picture frame
Modelling clay or mixed paper pulp
Clear adhesive
Shells
Twine, or smooth parcel string
Mixed wallpaper paste
Tissue paper
White emulsion paint
Acrylic paints

**Preparation**
1 Stick the hardboard frame to the picture frame.

2 Mould a starfish from modelling clay, or cut a cardboard starfish shape and build up the surface with paper pulp.

3 Stick the starfish at bottom left of the frame.

4 Stick the shells centre top and bottom right of the frame.

5 Using the glue nozzle, mark thin lines of adhesive on the frame where the string is to be.

6 Lay the string along the glue lines and lightly press down.

**Working the design**
7 When the adhesive is completely dry, brush paste over the entire frame. Brush pieces of tissue on to the frame so that the shells, starfish and string show in relief.

8 Paste the tissue edges over to the back of the frame. Add 2 more layers in the same way, making sure that the tissue edges are taken over to the back so that the frame edges are rounded off.

9 You may find that the starfish needs more layers of tissue.

Stick the hardboard frame to the picture frame.

Mark lines of adhesive for the string patterns.

**10** When the pasted tissue is dry, give the frame 2 coats of white emulsion paint. Leave to dry.

**11** Paint the frame pale blue and the starfish yellow. Brush yellow over the shells and along the string lines.

# Art Deco plate

*Papier mâché plates are strong and long-lasting and are ideal for displaying on a dresser or on the wall. They can safely be used for dry foods, fruit or sweets but should not be put into water.*

## Materials
Plate for a mould
Petroleum jelly
Newspaper torn into 4 × ½in (10 × 1cm) strips
Mixed wallpaper paste
Tissue paper
PVA adhesive
White emulsion paint
Acrylic paints

## Preparation
1 Smear the surface and edges of the plate with petroleum jelly.

## Working the design
2 Brush paste on to one side of the paper strips. Apply to the plate. Start at the edges and work towards the centre, overlapping the strips.

3 When the plate has a complete layer of paper, leave to dry.

4 Apply 5 more layers, leaving the work to dry between each application.

5 After the final layer, gently lift the paper shell from the plate. Trim the edges with sharp scissors.

6 Paste small pieces of tissue paper over the surface of the shell, taking the tissue over the edges. Then work the back of the shell.

7 Continue adding layers of pasted tissue paper until the paper plate feels thick and solid and the surface is smooth.

8 When the plate is completely dry, paint it with white emulsion paint.

9 Finally, decorate the plate with acrylic colours.

Paste newspaper strips to the plate mould, starting at the edges.

**Geometric design**

Measure and mark the middle of the plate. Draw lines dividing the plate into quarters. Divide the quarters making eighths. Divide the segments twice to make 32 lines radiating from the middle. Measure and mark 1in (2.5cm) in from the plate edge. Draw a line all round. Measure and mark a line ¾in (18mm) away and then a third line ½in (1cm) away. This makes a chequered border all round the plate. Paint alternate spaces black. For a different effect, paint the border in 4 or 5 bright colours, or paint a motif in each space on the white ground.

# Blue printed jug

*In this project, the papier mâché is worked over a long balloon and the finished jug is hand-printed with flowers. You could also cut motifs from flowered gift paper and stick them to the jug.*

## Materials
Inflated long balloon
Newspaper torn into small pieces
Mixed wallpaper paste
Thin card
Clear, sticky tape
Tissue paper
2 florist's stub wires
Masking tape
Acrylic paints
Plastic eraser
Sharp scalpel, crafts knife
PVA adhesive

## Preparation
**1** Stand the balloon in a mug to hold it steady while you work on it.

## Working the design
**2** Cover the top 8in (20cm) of the balloon with newspaper pieces dipped in water. Leave to dry, then repeat the process 5–6 times with pasted newspaper, leaving the work to dry between each application.

**3** Pop the balloon and gently pull it from the work.

**4** With a sharp knife, cut the rounded end off the paper shell. Trim the other end neatly.

**5** Measure across the paper shell and cut a circle of card to fit the base. Tape the base in place and then cover the join with pasted tissue, inside and out.

**6** Cut a triangular piece from the top edge of the jug. Cut a larger triangle of card, fold it and tape into the cutaway area for a pouring lip.

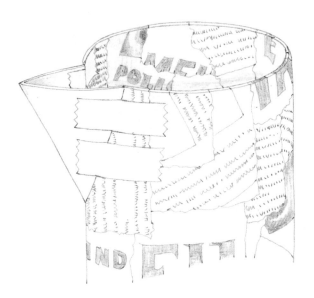
Fold a card triangle and tape in the cutaway area.

Cut the drawn motif in relief from the eraser.

**7 Handle:** Cut a strip of masking tape to the same length as the stub wires. Press the wires on to the sticky surface. Press another strip of tape on top.

**8** Bend the handle to shape and tape to the side of the jug.

**9** Cover the handle with strips of pasted tissue.

**10** Paste 2 layers of tissue all over the jug to smooth off the surface.

### Decoration
**11** Paint the jug with white emulsion paint. Then paint it with cream-coloured acrylic paint.

**12 Printing blocks:** Using a fine, fibre-tipped pen, copy the large flower on to the flat end of the eraser. Using a scalpel knife, carefully cut around the motif so that it stands in relief.

**13** Mix a little acrylic paint in a saucer. Dip in the printing block and print large flowers over the jug (see picture).

**14** When the large flowers have been printed, slice the top off the eraser and copy and cut the small flower motif. Print small flowers on the jug.

**15** Working in the same way, cut and print the stems and then, finally, the leaves.

**16** If the design appears to need some linking stems, these can be painted in using a fine brush.

**17** Paint a line round the jug rim.

**18** Give the jug a final coat of diluted PVA adhesive.

---

### Flower patterns
Choose a wallpaper printed with a small flower motif in a single colour on a white ground. Tear the wallpaper into small, circular pieces, about 1in (2.5cm) across. Paint the jug white. Paste the scraps to the jug, overlapping the edges. Varnish.

**Trace these motifs for eraser block printing.**

111

# Teddy bear

*Three large paper bags and shredded paper make this appealing bear. Children will love him, to sit on the bedside table, but grown-up bear lovers will treasure this Teddy.*

### Materials
3 large paper bags approximately 8 × 8in (20 × 20cm)
Shredded or torn-up newspaper
Clear adhesive tape
Mixed pulp (refer to Better Techniques)
Masking tape
PVA adhesive
Toy bear eyes, or beads
Acrylic paints
18in (45cm) satin ribbon, 1in (2.5cm) wide

### Preparation
1 Draw the leg and arm shapes on paper bags. Cut out as shown on the dotted lines.

2 Tape the cut edges of the shapes.

3 Stuff the 2 legs and 2 arms with torn-up newspaper.

4 Roll a 3in (7.5cm)-diameter ball of newspaper for the bear's head. Tape to hold the shape.

5 Stuff the remaining bag with paper for the bear's body. Use masking tape to shape the body.

6 Tape the head, arms and legs to the body.

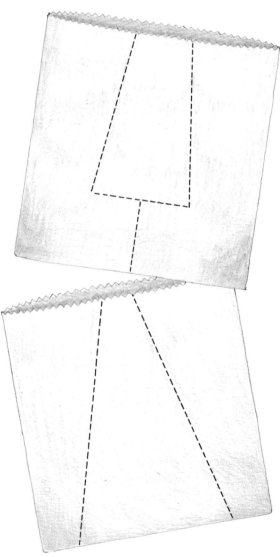

Tape the edges and stuff the leg with torn newspaper.

Draw the arms and legs on paper bags, cut out.

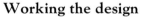

## Working the design

**7** Mix 2 cups of pulp with $\frac{3}{4}$ cup of PVA adhesive. Using a knife, spread the mixture all over the bear's body, head and limbs. Leave to dry.

**8** Mix more paper pulp and PVA. Working slowly, and a little at a time, build up the shape of the head and nose. Press the eyes into the head to leave indentations. Leave the modelling to dry between stages – do not try to do too much shaping at one time. Build up and shape the ears with blobs of pulp.

**9** Stick the eyes (or beads) into the indentations.

**10** Paint the bear with acrylic colours.

**11** Tie a ribbon bow round the bear's neck.

113

# Sitting duck

*Decoy ducks are popular as room accessories and this papier mâché model looks very authentic. The painted decoration is important if you are to achieve the right effect.*

### Materials
Large plastic shopping bag
Masking tape
Newspaper
Brown paper bag approximately 8in
     (20cm) square
Tissue paper
Mixed wallpaper paste
Thin cardboard
White emulsion paint
Acrylic paints
PVA adhesive

### Preparation
**1** Draw the wing and tail shapes on squared paper and cut from thin card.

**2** Fold up the corners of the plastic bag and tape. Stuff with crumpled newspaper. Tape the bag to form a pear shape.

**3** Cut a corner from the brown paper bag. Tape the cut edges closed. Fold over the opposite corner and tape down. Stuff with tissue paper. Tape the bag to form the duck's head. Crumple pieces of tissue paper and tape to the head to assist the shaping.

**4** Tape the head to the rounded end of the body.

**5** Tape the wings to the sides of the body, crossing the wing tips. Tape the two tails to the end of the body, the larger tail on top.

Smooth out the body bumps with tape.

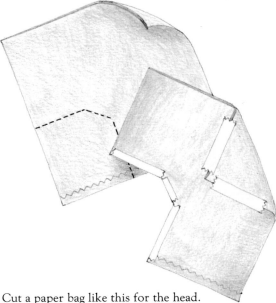

Cut a paper bag like this for the head. Tape the edges.

### Working the design
**6** Tear newspaper strips and paste them all over the duck. Leave to dry.

**7** Apply 3–4 layers in the same way, leaving each layer to dry before applying the next.

**8** The duck should feel 'solid' at this stage. Apply more layers of newspaper strips if necessary. Paste 3 layers of tissue over the duck to smooth the surface.

**9** Paint the duck with white emulsion paint.

**10** Working from the picture, decorate the duck.

**11** Give the duck a final coat of diluted PVA adhesive.

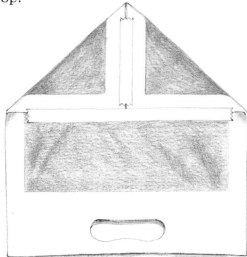

Tape up the corners of a shopping bag.

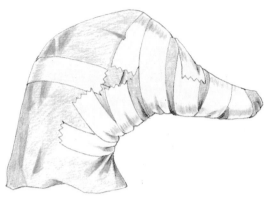

Shape the stuffed bag to a duck's head.

Draw patterns for the wings and tails.
Scale 1 sq = 1in (2.5cm).

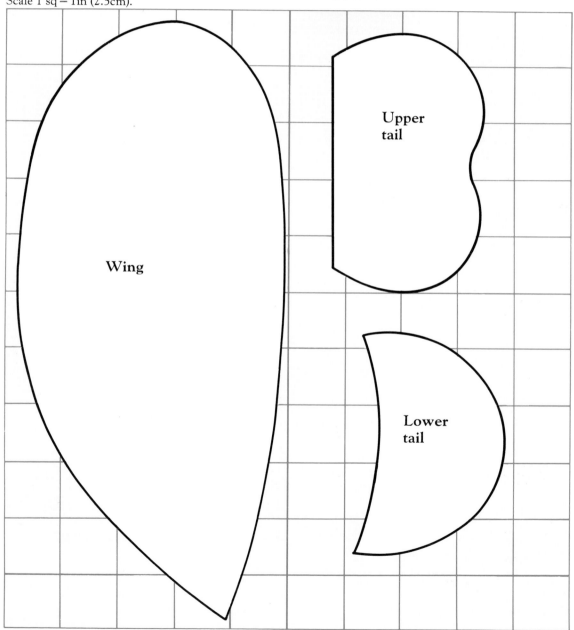

Wing

Upper tail

Lower tail

# Sleeping cat

*This dozing feline will rest by the fireside or by a chair. Although it looks complex, the cat is, in fact, very easy to make and is based on a paper bag and a plastic shopping bag.*

**Materials**
Large, brown paper bag
Plastic shopping bags
Tissue paper
Clear, sticky tape
Thin cardboard
Newspaper
Mixed wallpaper paste
White emulsion paint
Acrylic paints
PVA adhesive

**Preparation**
**1** Cut three corners from the paper bag and tape the edges. Stuff with the plastic bags.

**2** Crumple tissue paper into a ball for the head and tape to hold the shape.

Cut the corners from a paper bag and tape.

**3** Tape the head to the paper bag body. Crumple some more tissue and tape beside the head to round off the body so that the shape of a curled-up cat is obtained. (Refer to the picture.)

**4** Trace the ear shape and cut 2 from card. Tape to the head on the long edges.

**Working the design**
**5** Paste newspaper strips and apply a layer all over the cat. Leave to dry. Apply 3 more layers, leaving each one to dry before working the next.

**6** Apply two layers of pasted tissue to smooth the surface.

**7** Paint the entire cat with white emulsion.

**8** Decorate the cat with acrylic colours. When dry, give a final coat of diluted PVA adhesive.

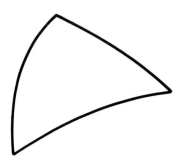

**Trace this ear shape, cut 2 from card.**

Tape the head and crumpled tissue to the body.

# Black and white cat

*Cat-lovers will treasure this life-like model – it makes an ideal gift for both children and adults. The basic structure is a plastic soft drinks bottle shaped with newspaper-stuffed plastic bags.*

**Materials**
2 litre plastic soft drinks bottle
Plastic covered garden wire
Florist's stub wires
Clear adhesive tape
Plastic shopping bags
Newspaper
Wallpaper paste
Tissue paper
PVA adhesive
Acrylic paints

**Preparation**
1 Cut the bottom 4in (10cm) from the plastic bottle.

2 Trace the outlines for the wire armatures. Bend the thicker wire to the shapes of the tracings.

3 Fit the two wire shapes together and tape the wire ends to the bottle.

4 With thin wire, build up the head, twisting the wire round the thicker wire to hold the shape.

5 Stuff plastic bags with newspaper and arrange the bags over the bottle to shape the cat's body. Tape in place.

6 Roll a sheet of newspaper diagonally to form the tail. Tape to the body.

7 Cut 2 pieces of card $3 \times 4\frac{1}{2}$in ($7.5 \times 11$cm) for legs. Roll into 1in (2.5cm)-diameter tubes. Stuff the bottom end of the tubes with screwed up paper for the feet. Flatten the other end of the tubes. Tape the legs to the body.

**Trace these outlines for the head shape.**

**Working the design**

**8** Cover the entire cat with pasted strips of newspaper. Leave to dry.

**9 Shaping the face** Paste larger strips of newspaper and apply to the face to build up the muzzle. Take your time over this stage and do not try to do too much shaping in one session. Leave the work to dry out between each application.

**10** Stand the finished cat on a piece of card and draw round the base. Cut out the shape and glue to the underside of the cat.

**11** Paste pieces of tissue paper all over the cat and base to smooth the surface.

**12** Brush 2 coats of PVA adhesive over the cat.

**13** Trace the eye shapes on thin card and use them to position the eyes. When you have them in the right place, trace round the outlines and paint in the eyes.

Fit the wire shapes together, tape to the bottle. Tape newspaper-stuffed plastic bags to the bottle to shape the body.

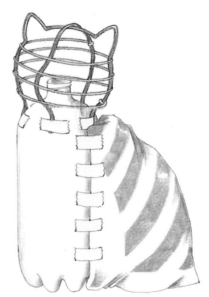

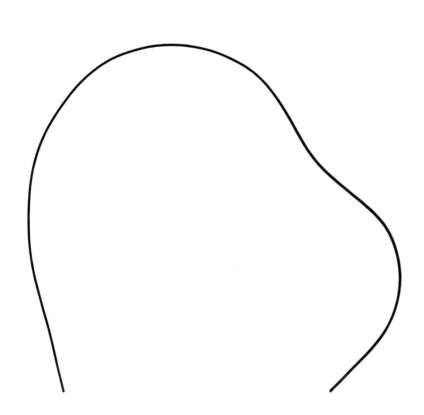

# Serviette rings

*Decorated with paper cut-outs, papier mâché*
*serviette rings make acceptable gifts for family and friends –*
*if you can bear to part with them.*

**Materials**
Cardboard tubes (refer to Better
   Techniques)
Mixed wallpaper paste
Newspaper torn into strips
Tissue paper
PVA adhesive
Giftwrap, magazine illustrations, rub-on
   initials etc
White emulsion paint
Fine sandpaper
Water-soluble paste
Acrylic paint; gold paint
Matt varnish

**Preparation**
1 Make cardboard tubes of the desired
dimensions.

**Working the design**
2 Wrap the ring with narrow strips of
pasted newspaper until the edges are
rounded. Leave the work to dry between
layers.

3 Apply 2–3 layers of pasted tissue, to
smooth off the surface.

4 When the papier mâché is dry, give the
ring 2 coats of white emulsion paint.
When dry, rub down with fine sandpaper
until the surfaces on the inside and
outside are quite smooth.

5 Paint the ring with acrylic colours.

6 If the ring has an uneven surface after
painting, rub down again to smoothness.

7 Using fine, curve-bladed nail scissors,
cut motifs from thin paper. Paste round
the ring using water-soluble paste.

8 Press the motifs with a finger tip to
squeeze out any excess paste. Clean the
edges with a dampened cotton wool bud.
Leave to dry.

9 Spray the ring with fixative and leave
to dry.

10 Using a good-quality, soft-bristled
brush, apply a thin coat of varnish to the
outside of the ring. Suspend the ring on a
spoon handle to dry.

11 Apply more coats of varnish to the
ring, allowing each coat to dry before
applying the next, until the edges of the
motifs cannot be felt with a finger nail.
Between 5–6 coats may be needed.

12 Finally, varnish the inside of the ring.

Press a blob of Plasticine to the spoon handle, rest
the serviette ring on it to dry.

124

# Man-in-the-moon

*Hang the moon where there is a draught so that it turns in the current of air – or suspend the decoration where it is reflected in a mirror. For Christmas, you might make some matching silver stars.*

## Materials
12in (30cm) square of thick card
1 cup of mixed paper pulp (refer to
    Better Techniques)
Tissue paper
Mixed wallpaper paste
Black acrylic paint
Silver paint
Silver reel wire

## Preparation
1  Cut a 10in (25cm) circle from the card.

2  Draw the moon's face from the graph pattern and transfer to the card. Cut out.

## Working the design
3  Spread a thin layer over one side of the moon shape. Leave to dry.

4  Spread a layer of pulp on the other side and leave to dry.

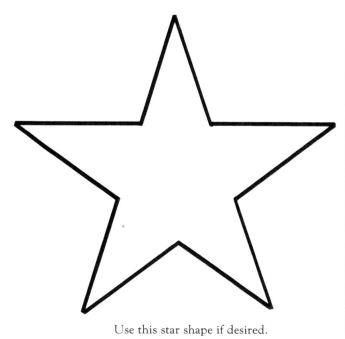

Use this star shape if desired.

**5** With the face looking to the right, use pulp to build up the features. Do not attempt too much modelling in one session. Take your time and allow each application to dry before starting again.

**6** If cracks appear, fill them with more pulp. If the moon begins to warp as it dries, put weights on the ends.

**7** Finally, apply 2 layers of pasted tissue paper to smooth the surface.

**8** Paint the moon black on both sides. When dry, dip a piece of cloth in silver paint and rub all over the raised surfaces so that the black shows through. Pierce a hole at the top of the moon and thread silver wire through. Twist the end.

**Working with graph patterns**
Making your own patterns from graph patterns is not difficult although it can look daunting at first sight. You need the following materials and equipment for pattern making.

● Dressmakers' squared paper: this comes in different scales. Choose the one specified in the pattern.
● Tape measure and ruler.
● Medium-soft pencils.
● A flexible, plastic ruler for drawing curves.

**To begin:** Study the pattern and count the number of squares, first across the top edge and then down one side. Check with the scale. This tells you the dimensions of the area you will need on squared pattern paper. Draw this area.

With a pencil, number the squares on the graph pattern, across the top edge and then down one side. Number the squares on the squared pattern paper in the same way.

Using a ruler, and working from the graph pattern, copy any straight pattern lines. Still working from the graph pattern, mark any key points on the curved lines. Join up these points to complete the outline of the pattern.

Man-in-the-moon: scale 1 sq = 1in (2.5cm).

# Valentine keepsakes

*Make a lace-edged heart to send to someone you love on this special day. The hearts can be hung for a wall decoration or will make an attractive accessory on a side table.*

**Materials**
Thin card
Mixed paper pulp (refer to Better Techniques)
Newspaper
Tissue paper
Mixed wallpaper paste
Acrylic paints
Gathered lace edging
Paper lace doily
Ribbon

**Preparation**
1 Trace the heart shape and cut from thin card.

**Working the design**
2 Build up the heart with paper pulp. Smooth off the surface and leave to dry.

3 When dry, apply small pieces of pasted newspaper all over the heart. Leave to dry.

4 Apply 3 layers of pasted tissue all over the heart, leaving each layer to dry before working the next.

5 Paint the heart on both sides.

6 Stick lace round the heart, joining the ends at the top. Cut pieces from the paper lace doily and stick over the edge of the lace.

7 Tie a small ribbon bow and stick to the front of the heart. Make a ribbon loop and stick to the top of the heart, just behind the ribbon bow.

**Trace the heart shape, cut from card.**

# Mini-hamper

*What could be more exciting than a miniature hamper, full of ribbon-tied tiny boxes spilling out onto the party table? The boxes could contain little gifts for going-home presents for your guests.*

## Materials
Pattern paper
Thin card
Clear adhesive tape or quick-drying
   adhesive
Giftwrap papers with a small pattern
Narrow ribbons
Wicker basket with a hinged lid
Tissue paper

## Preparation
**1 Boxes** Trace the box pattern on paper. Transfer to thin card and cut out as many boxes as required. Score along the broken lines and fold the box sides and lid. Tape or stick the tabs to form the boxes. Insert small gifts at this stage if required.

### More ideas
Use the hamper centrepiece as a 'lucky dip' for your guests. Invite them to choose a parcel – both children and adults love a surprise. If a larger basket can be obtained, try painting it gold and then fill it with gold-wrapped gifts. Leave the lid slightly open. From each gift, trail a ribbon to each place setting and stick a tiny card with the guest's name to the end.

   As an alternative to boxes, the hamper could be filled with special chocolates and candies.

**Trace the box pattern from this diagram. Score on the broken lines.**

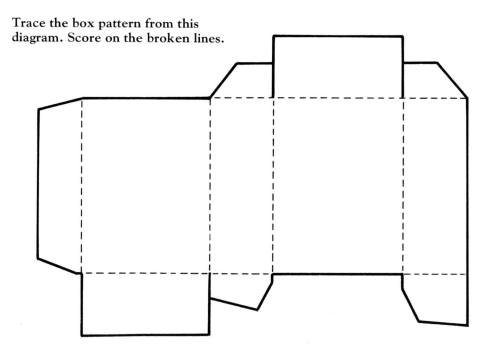

**2** Wrap the boxes in giftwrap paper and tie with narrow ribbons.

**Working the design**
**3** Shred the tissue paper. Put a layer of shreds in the bottom of the basket.

**4** Top the tissue paper shreds with wrapped boxes. Some boxes could have tiny sprays of silk flowers added, tucked under the ribbons.

133

# Party poppies

*Bright paper poppies make a cheerful display for a teenage party. For unusual containers, stand the poppies in empty blue or green mineral water bottles.*

**Materials**
Tracing paper
Double-sided crepe paper (red, yellow or orange)
Black watercolour paint or crayon
Florists' stub wires, 12–15in (30–37.5cm) long
Cotton wool
Florists' binding wire
Black crêpe paper
Florists' green stem tape

**Preparation**
**1** Trace the poppy petal pattern on folded paper. Cut out and use the pattern to cut 6 petals from crêpe paper with the direction arrow lying along the grain.

**Working the design**
**2** Curve and cup each petal by holding it between thumbs and forefingers and stretching from the centre outwards. Using black paint, brush strokes from the bottom end of each petal.

**3** Cut a $1 \times 8$in ($2.5 \times 20$cm) strip of black paper on the cross grain. Cut a $\frac{1}{2}$in (1cm) fringe on the grain along one edge.

**4 Assembling the poppy** Bend a hook on one end of a stub wire. Thread binding wire through the hook and twist it round the stem. Leave a wire end.

**5** Cover the hook with cotton wool. Bind it securely with the wire.

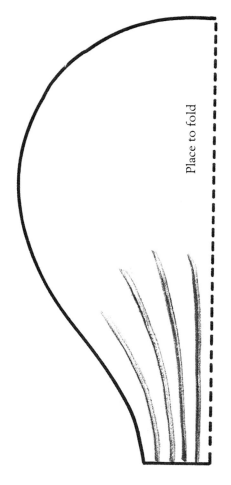

Place to fold

**Trace this petal on folded pattern paper.**

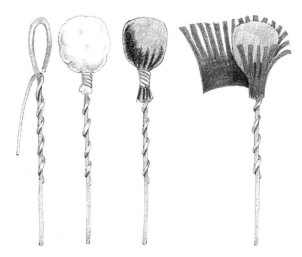

Bend a hook on the stub wire and thread binding wire through. Cover the hook with cotton wool. Wire the black fringe round.

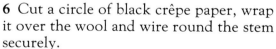

**6** Cut a circle of black crêpe paper, wrap it over the wool and wire round the stem securely.

**7** Gather the black paper fringe in the fingers and wire this round the outside of the black poppy centre.

**8** Take each petal in turn, pleat the bottom end and wire round the poppy centre, overlapping each petal slightly.

**9** Cover the stem with stem tape, twisting the stem in your fingers as you work. Arrange the poppies in a container.

**10** If you like, cut leaves from two-tone green crêpe paper and tape to the stem as you cover it.

135

# Pretty place cards

*Decorative place cards can set the mood of your party. Amusing, colourful shapes and figures delight children while festive-looking motifs create a Christmas party theme.*

### Materials
Good-quality, smooth-surfaced coloured
  cartridge paper
Sticky-backed coloured paper
Sticky-back stars
Felt-tipped pens
You will also need a metal edged ruler,
  sharp crafts knife, scoring tool and
  sharp scissors

### Preparation
**1** Measure and mark the dimension of the place cards on the sheet of card. Measure accurately and make sure corners are exactly square. An ideal size for a place card, folded, is 4 × 3in (10 × 7.5cm), so measure rectangles 8 × 3in (20 × 7.5cm). However, place cards can be any shape or size you desire.

**2** Measure and mark the middle of the paper across the width. Holding the ruler along the marks, draw the scoring tool across. This breaks the surface tension of the paper and the place card will fold cleanly.

### Working the designs
**3 Hallowe'en party** Make the card from black paper. Score and fold. Trace the pumpkin motif and transfer onto orange paper. Cut out. Stick the pumpkin to the front of the folded card.

**4 Easter party** Make the card from green paper. Score and fold. Trace the egg shape and transfer to yellow paper. Cut out the egg. Trace and cut out the ribbon bow from white paper. Stick the bow on the egg and colour it with felt-tipped pens. Stick the egg to the front of the card.

**5 Christmas party** Make the card from dark blue paper. Score and fold. Trace the candle and cut the candle itself from red paper. Cut out the larger, yellow flame and the smaller, orange flame. Stick the orange flame on the yellow flame, then stick the flame behind the candle. Stick the candle to the card. Decorate with stick-on stars.

**Quick menu cards**
Save seasonal or occasional greeting cards and trim the picture to fit into a two-fold window card blank. Handwrite the menu inside the card in gold pen. Add the date of the occasion at the bottom corner.

**Trace these patterns for place cards.**

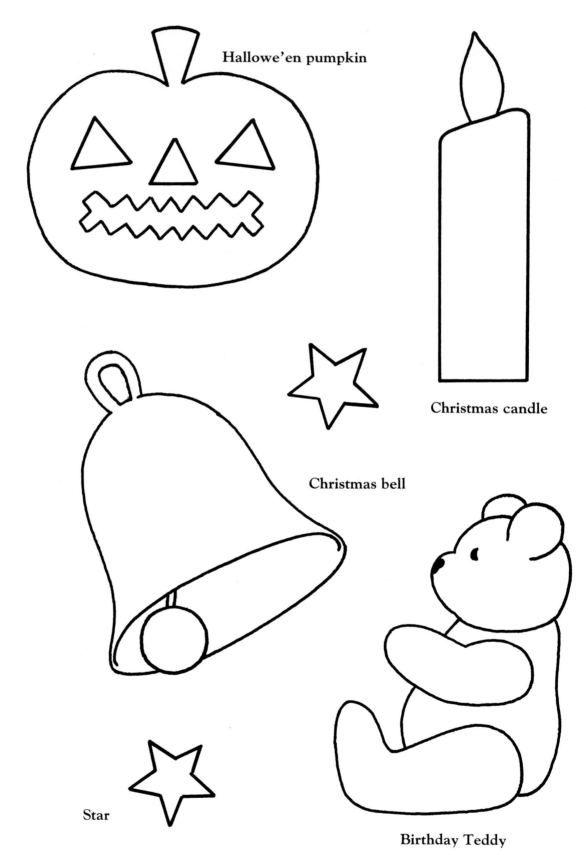

Hallowe'en pumpkin

Christmas candle

Christmas bell

Star

Birthday Teddy

**Wedding or Christening swan**

 Stars

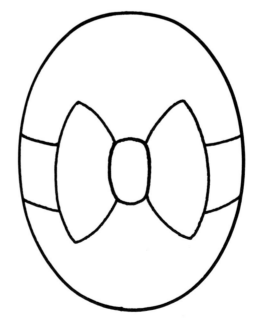

**Easter egg**

**Sticky-backed paper**
This easy-to-use crafts paper is usually sold in mixed-colour packets of 8in (20cm) square sheets. To reproduce a design, first trace each area of colour separately. Transfer the shapes onto the right side of the coloured paper, using typist's carbon paper. Cut out the shapes with a small pair of scissors. Arrange the pieces on the work surface, so that you can see which pieces should overlap. Dampen the back of the shapes with a moistened piece of cotton wool (use a cotton bud for very tiny pieces). Position the shapes on the chosen background.

# Little boxes

*Small decorated boxes have dozens of uses in party decorations. Apart from being used to contain sweets for the table, they are also perfect containers for Christmas tree gifts.*

**Materials**
Matchbox trays (or make your own
   boxes)
Good quality, stiff card for boxes
Quick-drying adhesive
Patterned giftwrap
Spray adhesive
Lacy paper doilies
Stiff gift ribbon
Decorations such as narrow satin ribbon,
   lace edging, silk flowers etc

**Preparation**
1 If you are making boxes, draw the
diagram on white card and cut out. Score
along the broken lines, fold up the box
and tape the corners.

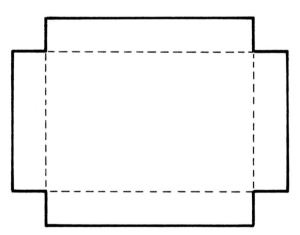

Draw this box tray pattern to any size desired.

**Working the design**
2 Stand the box on the wrong side of the
giftwrap paper and draw round the base.
Turn the box on its side (still in the same
place) and mark the depth of the side on
the paper.

3 Draw all four box sides onto the base
outline. Add ¼in (6mm) to the long edges.
Add ¼in (6mm) to the sides of the
corners.

4 Cut out the shape. Snip into the
corners. Press folds into the paper along
the marked lines.

5 Smooth out the paper shape. Spray
adhesive onto the wrong side. Stand the
card box on the paper and fold up the
sides, overlapping the corners for a
smooth finish. Turn the top edge to the
inside of the box.

6 Cut pieces of edging from the doily
and stick them round the inside top edge
of the box, so that the frilly edge shows.

**Finishing and assembly**
7 Cut a piece of stiff gift ribbon, crinkle
ribbon (untwisted) or cord for a handle.
Staple the ends to the long sides of the
box.

8 Crumple a little tissue paper (or cut
tissue paper shreds) and put a layer at the
bottom of the box. Add small gifts,
sweets etc. Decorate with ribbons or
flowers as desired.

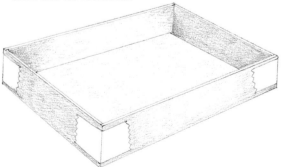

Tape up the corners.

# Candy cones

*For a really quick and easy table decoration, you cannot beat paper cones. These have been filled with delicious sweets but you can also use cones for dried flower holders.*

**Materials**
Patterned giftwrap, metallic giftwrap
Double-sided tape
Gift tie ribbons
Sequins, buttons

**Preparation**
1 Cut an 8in (20cm) square of giftwrap paper for each cone.

**Working the design**
2 Roll the paper from the bottom left corner to form a cone.

3 Fasten the overlap with double sided tape. Flatten the cone slightly so that the point is central. Turn up the other end and tape flat.

**4 Decorating the cones** Stick three buttons of different colours along the front of a pink cone. Stick four heart-shaped sequins along the front of a yellow cone. Make a ribbon rosette and stick it to a green metallic cone. Cut a piece of pink gift tie ribbon and cut the ends diagonally. Stick to a striped paper cone. Decorate with a tiny bow of pink ribbon.

5 Crumple a piece of soft tissue and push it into the cones to hold the shape.

6 Lay the cones on the table and fill them with sweets.

**Ribbon roses**
Although tiny ribbon roses can be purchased, you might like to try making your own for decorating candy cones and baskets. Cut a 6in (15cm) length of ½in (1cm)-wide gift ribbon. Working towards you, roll the right hand end into a tight tube (A). Hold the bottom of the tube in your right hand, very firmly. With your other hand, fold the ribbon away from you diagonally (B). Then roll the tube onto the diagonal fold and keep rolling until the ribbon lies straight again. Make another diagonal fold and roll the tube onto it (C). Keep doing this until all the ribbon length has been used up (D). Take the ribbon end under the rosette and catch it to the underside with a few stitches – or a touch of quick-drying glue.

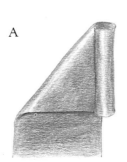
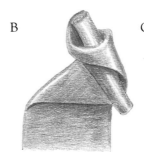

A    B    C    D

# Better Techniques

*This chapter brings together all you need to know about paper, card, paste and paint. Here you will discover the best methods for creating perfect pieces of papier mâché and découpage and gain a wealth of knowledge about working with paper.*

**PAPIER MACHE**
**MATERIALS AND EQUIPMENT**
Papier mâché can be worked in various ways. Two techniques are in this book, layering and pulp work. The two most important materials you will be using are paper and adhesive.

**PAPER**
Newspaper has been used for most of the projects in this book but it is by no means the only paper that can be used. Almost any type of strong paper can be used for the foundation work – computer print-out paper, discarded letters and envelopes, typing paper – anything that comes to hand and which you can obtain in quantity. Old newspapers are, of course, a traditional favourite for papier mâché as these are readily available, cost nothing and are easy to handle. In this book, newspaper has also been used to make paper pulp.
**Kitchen roll paper** This is useful for building up work quickly. If kitchen paper is alternated with newspaper in layering, you can see if the surface being worked has been completely covered.
**Tissue paper** When layering or modelling is completed, tissue paper is used to smooth off the surface ready for undercoat painting. Tissue can also be used to add texture to a surface. Soft, paper handkerchiefs can also be used for the final layer.

**Decorative papers** Giftwrap can be used for decorating an object, either torn into strips for layering or for motifs. Tissue and crêpe paper are available in wide colour ranges and interesting effects can be achieved with these. Scraps of coloured paper from magazine pages often provide unusual patterns and textures which can be used as a decorative finish.

**CARDBOARD**
In this book, cardboard has been used to make basic structures and for surface decoration. In every instance, the cardboard has been throw-away waste.

Cardboard throw-away waste is ideal for papier mâché. Corrugated card, transit cartons, cereal boxes and fruit packing are all easily available.

**Thin cardboard** Where this has been recommended, cardboard of the weight and flexibility of cereal packets is required.

**Thick cardboard** When rigid card is required, cartons used for transit packaging of canned goods etc have been used. Suitable cartons are usually obtainable from supermarkets.

**Corrugated card** This is also freely available from supermarkets.

**Pulped paper packing** This useful material is used in packing fruit and comes pre-formed to take the shape of the fruit.

## ADHESIVES FOR PAPIER MACHE

**Wallpaper paste** Cellulose wallpaper paste comes as granules which are mixed with water. Mix paste beforehand in order to allow time for the grains to swell. Use it at the strongest proportion and dilute it as required. Some wallpaper pastes have a fungicide in them and thus may not be suitable for children to use. Wash your hands frequently when working with these pastes.

**PVA adhesive** PVA is a multi-purpose, easy-to-use adhesive which can be used both as a glue and a varnish. Although white, PVA dries transparent and, as a finish, gives a glossy, protective surface. It can be used full strength or diluted with water.

**Latex adhesives** This is thick and white and comes in jars or tubes. It is specifically for sticking fabric, paper and card but should be used very sparingly.

**Clear adhesive** For working with paper and card, a clear, quick-drying, non-trailing adhesive is essential.

**Water soluble paste** This is available in jars and squeeze containers and is semi-opaque. It is safe for children to use, under supervision, and spills or smears can be removed with water.

**Flour and water paste** This is ideal for paper mâché layering and works as well as wallpaper paste. If salt is added, the paste will keep for several days. Between sessions, cover the paste and put in the refrigerator.

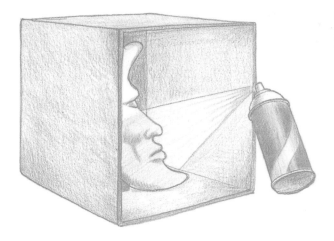

Use a large cardboard carton as a paint-spraying booth. Prop the object at an angle if required.

**Spray adhesive** allows you to spread adhesive over a large area of paper without dampening the surface. Spray adhesive should be used either in the open air or in a confined space (such as a spraying booth made from a cardboard box).

**Flour and water paste**
Mix plain flour and water together to a thick cream. Pour on boiling water, stirring. The paste will turn translucent and thicken. Dilute as required. Stir in a large spoon of salt to 6 cups of paste to keep it from hardening. Flour and water paste will keep in the refrigerator for several days.

### Papier mâché pastes

For papier mâché, mix wallpaper paste to full strength. The drying time is a bit longer, however, with a wet adhesive such as this. Undiluted PVA can be added to the paste to stiffen it slightly, and to speed drying time. PVA can also be used on its own, diluted with water to a stiff cream consistency. A PVA-only solution produces papier mâché with a light, almost plastic, feel to it.

## PAINTS, DYES AND VARNISHES

Acrylic paints, which are water-mixable, have been used for decorating all the projects in this book. These paints dry quickly with a silky, waterproof finish. The shade ranges are large, and frosted colours are also available. Wash brushes immediately after use because acrylic paint dries hard in a very short time. There are special finishing varnishes for acrylic paints.

Other paints used for crafts include poster paints, water colours and designer gouache. Model maker's enamel paints and multi-purpose metallic paints can also be used.

**Emulsion paint** Water-based white paint is used as an undercoat before decoration.

**Gold and silver** paints and spray paints are needed for some projects.

**Varnish** for finishing and protecting work can be gloss, satin or matt finish.

**Paint brushes** should include a range of water-colour brushes and small, household decorating brushes.

**Dyeing pulp** Cold water dyes or fabric dyes can be used for colouring pulp and interesting effects are possible. The dye colour will lighten on drying.

## OTHER MATERIALS AND EQUIPMENT

### Tapes

For papier mâché, you will need masking tape, clear, sticky tape and brown paper strip tape.

### Sandpaper

Fine sandpaper is used to smooth rough edges on layered and pulp papier mâché.

### Plastic-covered garden wire

This is used for making armatures under papier mâché.

All the basic equipment needed for papier mâché, bowls, spoons, knives, buckets, cups and mugs etc, can be found in the average kitchen (see Check list).

### Cutting tools

**Knives:** You will need two kinds of craft knives: a heavy duty knife, like a Stanley knife or an X-acta knife for cutting thick card, and a small knife, preferably a scalpel, for thin card and paper. Use straight blades, as these suit most tasks and replace them often for the best results. Needless to say, these knives require care when in use. You should always cut straight lines by lining up the knife against a firm straight edge. Use a metal rule for this rather than a plastic or wood ruler, as these materials can easily catch in the blade.

**Scissors:** You will need several pairs of sharp scissors. Have a pair of fairly small, easy-to-handle scissors with straight, pointed blades for most cutting jobs, a longer broad-bladed pair for general cutting and manicure scissors with curved blades for cutting round intricate shapes.

### Drawing aids

Drawing aids required include a pair of compasses, a set square and a ruler with small measurement markings. You will also need paper clips, a stapler, a pencil sharpener and a selection of HB and soft pencils, coloured pencils and felt tipped pens. A good quality eraser is helpful.

If you are constantly using quick-dry glue, choose a nail which fits tightly into the tube nozzle. Knock the nail through wood then fit the nozzle on the nail when the glue is not in use.

## BASIC TECHNIQUES
### Layering method

When you are using a dish or bowl-shaped mould, protect the work surface with newspaper then invert the mould over a suitable prop, like a can or mug – any object tall enough to raise the mould off the work surface and keep it stable.

Prepare the mould or structure. Tear paper into small strips about ½in (1cm)

Tear newspaper into long strips, then tear the strips into small squares and rectangles.

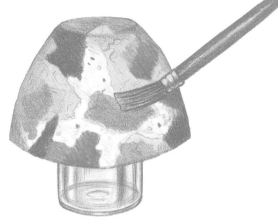

Rest the mould on a jar or can to raise it above the surface.

wide × 2in (5cm) long. This size strip will mould well round most curves. (For smaller or larger projects adapt the strip size.) As a guide, the strips should adhere to the mould without pleating or distorting.

Put some paste in a shallow bowl or dish. Start at the top of the greased

**Preparing moulds**

It is necessary to lubricate the mould before applying paper strips so that the finished papier mâché can be removed easily. Smear the mould surface liberally with petroleum jelly. If it is necessary to remove the papier mâché at any time during the drying process, re-grease the mould before replacing the work.

As an alternative method, dampen the first layer of strips instead of pasting them. The shell will then slip from the mould without difficulty.

mould. Use water only to dampen the strips and smooth each one in place, overlapping the edges slightly, to build a layer reaching downwards to the outside edge. Allow the strips to overlap the edge slightly as this can be trimmed later. Apply a second layer of strips, this time using paste and work the strips in the other direction. This helps to build a firm, strong web. Paint paste over the surface and smooth with your hands to remove any air bubbles. Do this after applying each layer of strips. Add another layer of glued strips, working downwards in the same direction as the first layer. Continue in this way until the layers are thick enough to hold the shape.

When you are working with newspaper strips, it is sometimes difficult to see whether you have completely covered the mould. If you use a different paper – such as kitchen roll paper – for alternate layers, you will be able to see when a layer has been completed.

148

Use a different paper for alternate layers. This helps to see when a layer has been completed.

## Check list
### Layering method
Paper, torn into strips
Mixed wallpaper paste
PVA adhesive
Paste container
Moulds
Petroleum jelly
Tissue paper
White emulsion paint
Household paint brushes
Varnish
Spoons for mixing
Crafts knives
Scissors
Metal-edged rule

### Pulp method
Paper
Bucket
Fabric conditioner
Whiting or ground chalk
Mixed wallpaper paste
Linseed oil
Slotted spoon
Saucepan
Blender
Fine-mesh sieve
Petroleum jelly
Blunt knives, spoons, tools etc for modelling

## Drying papier mâché
Papier mâché can take several days to dry so be patient if you want successful results. Keep the mould on the prop, and leave the work to dry naturally in a warm, airy place.

## Fine finish
Some pieces may require a smooth finish before painting. When the last layer of newspaper pieces has dried, tear white tissue paper into small pieces and paste all over the surface. Leave to dry, then apply another layer. A third layer may be necessary if the newspaper surface was rather rough.

## Removing work from the mould
To unmould a bowl shape, gently insert a thin knife, such as a palette knife, between the bowl and the mould and slide round to break any vacuum which may have formed. Gently twist the bowl and ease the papier mâché away and place on a work surface. Trim the uneven edge with scissors, or leave it in its natural state if you prefer. Check for any thin patches and build these up with extra strips. Leave to dry. Smooth any uneven patches with sandpaper.

Loosen the paper shell from the mould with a palette knife.

149

Trim the edges of the shell with scissors.

## Working intricate shapes

If the structure you are working on has protruding corners or curves, cut down on the number of newspaper layers and work more final layers with tissue paper. Bowls or plates with a decorative edge, for instance, will retain their edges if narrow strips of tissue are pasted over them. Use the bristles of the paste brush to work pasted tissue into crevices and corners. Brushing pasted tissue can also be used to create a decorative finish. Tear fairly large pieces of tissue, paste the surface of the piece liberally and then pick up the tissue on the brush. As you paste it into place, allow creases and folds to form.

## Work surface

The work surface is important. This should be at a good working height, flat and stable. You will require a protective surface to use over the work top, to protect it from cuts and scratches when using crafts knives. A sheet of thick card or board is a suitable protection but should be replaced frequently as the surface will become pitted from successive knife cuts.

## Pulp papier mâché

The material used for this technique is usually made from torn newspaper boiled up with water and with adhesive added. Other types of paper can be used instead of newspaper – copy paper, typing paper, scrap notepaper etc. The finished pulp is slippery in texture and rather wet to the touch. Paper pulp is modelled with the fingers in a similar way to clay. It can be worked over or inside a mould or it can be modelled over a base to build up a surface or design. The secret of successful pulp work is to let the work dry very slowly.

When using a mould, smear petroleum jelly over the entire area. Spoon the pulp into the mould and press it well down to ensure a compact layer.

A drying period of several days should be allowed. Avoid using any means of speeding up the drying process as this may cause the papier mâché to crack or distort. If small cracks do appear while drying, fill these with more pulp, smoothing off the surface, then replace the papier mâché to dry once again.

When you are building up an area, such as features on a face or a decoration on a frame or dish, model by applying the pulp slowly. Allow each layer to dry before continuing the work.

Jelly moulds with interesting shapes are ideal for making pulp models. Press in the pulp firmly.

## PAPER PULP

### Materials

6 double sheets of newspaper (or similar quantity of other white paper)

¼ cup fabric conditioner

7 large spoons of whiting or ground chalk

6 large spoons mixed wallpaper paste

2 medium-sized spoons linseed oil

4 medium-sized spoons PVA adhesive

Large saucepan

### Preparation

Tear the paper into small pieces no larger than ⅝in (15mm) square. Put the paper into the bucket and cover with water. Add the fabric conditioner. Leave to soak for 12 hours.

### Method

Pour water and paper into a large saucepan and bring to a boil. Simmer for 30 minutes. The paper will begin to break up. If a dark scum rises to the top of the water, skim this off. Leave the mixture to cool. Working in batches, mix, using the blender. Strain the pulp into a sieve and press with the back of a spoon to remove as much water as possible. Transfer the strained pulp to a large mixing bowl. Stirring well, mix in the whiting and wallpaper paste, then the linseed oil and PVA adhesive. Mix thoroughly. The pulp is ready for use.

Dried paper pulp can be purchased, requiring only the addition of cold water. This is easy to use and ideal for children where only a small amount of pulp may be needed at a session. You may also find it useful when working on a modelling project over several days, mixing only what is needed each day.

### Decorating papier mâché

After the last layer of smoothing tissue has been applied and has dried out, give the piece a thin coat of white emulsion paint and leave to dry. You may decide to apply 2 coats if the surface requires it. Acrylic paints, which are water-mixable and quick-drying, are ideal for painting papier mâché items but modeller's enamels, poster colours and even household paints can also be used. The painted decoration can be varnished with clear, polyurethane varnish or given a coat of water-diluted PVA adhesive. If the item is to hold liquid (such as a vase) then 3–4 coats of varnish should be applied both inside and outside.

If you cannot draw or paint, découpage is an ideal technique for decorating papier mâché. Paint the piece in a single colour. Cut motifs from colour magazines or from giftwrap. Paste them to the surface, using a water-soluble paste. Spray varnish all over. Leave to dry then apply several thin coats of varnish to the surface, leaving each coat to dry thoroughly before applying the next, until the paper edges cannot be felt with a finger nail. This is a very hard-wearing finish for items that will be handled a great deal.

To paint paper beads, thread them on a knitting needle, support the needle across mugs or jars.

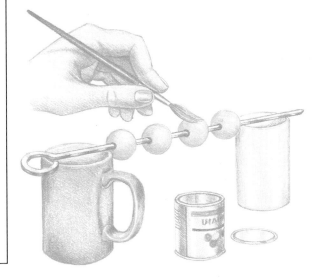

## DECOUPAGE
## MATERIALS AND EQUIPMENT

Everywhere you look there are printed papers that can be used for découpage, such as magazines and catalogues, sweet papers and food wrappers, postcards and greeting cards. Use old music sheets or old maps and drawings. Even a photocopy can provide a sharp black and white image.

Use flowers and seed packets to decorate garden objects, and food labels for trays.

You can use images from magazines, catalogues, sweet papers, food wrappers and cards.

Pick a theme that highlights the item you are decorating. Use flowers and seed packets to decorate garden objects, or food labels for trays and canisters for cooks. Alternatively, make an attractive découpage picture of holiday souvenirs.

The two most common souces of découpage material are giftwrap paper and old-fashioned decals, which are reminiscent of the Victorian decals – découpage was a popular craft at that time. Giftwrap paper can be found in many designs, so it's a good source if you want a particular look or motif. The best

papers for découpage are the paper sheets; foil papers are difficult to use.

Decals are bought by the sheet and provide unusual shapes and motifs that are easy to release from their backgrounds. They are useful when you want an old-fashioned look.

Decals are bought by the sheet and provide unusual shapes and motifs.

Thick paper such as greetings cards and cartons can be thinned down to make it easier to use. Soak the back of the whole card with a wet cloth until a layer of paper can be peeled away.

Thin papers can be strengthened (essential for 3-D découpage) by sticking them to plain typing or cartridge paper with spray adhesive.

## FIXING THE PATTERNED PAPERS

Spray fixative is available in either a matt or gloss finish. This is a useful way of sealing unstable papers, such as music sheets, doileys or magazine pages before they are used for découpage. Fixative prevents the paper from yellowing and will help seal colours. It will also prevent paper that is printed on both sides, such as magazine pages, from becoming transparent when coated with adhesive.

Spray matt or gloss fixative to seal unstable papers, such as music sheets.

## VARNISHES

Découpage is finished with several coats of varnish which seal the surface. In true découpage, coats of varnish should be applied until the edge of the shapes cannot be felt, but on small objects several coats will give the desired effect.

### Polyurethane clear wood varnish

This versatile varnish is available in matt, satin or gloss finishes. Matt varnish will give a flat even finish; the satin, a slight sheen, while gloss varnish will give a high shine to the finished article. Choose from either a clear or a tinted varnish, which will change the look of the découpage, giving it a sheen of colour or a wood effect.

### Artists' acrylic picture varnish

Similar to polyurethane varnish, this specialist type is more expensive but will not yellow with age. This varnish is also available as a spray.

### Poster and watercolour varnish

This is another specialist varnish, which gives a high gloss finish when applied over watercolour paints and papers.

### PAINTS

The most common paints used under découpage are household emulsion or artists' acrylic paints, but different paint effects can be applied to a surface before adding the cut-out shapes and it's worth experimenting before deciding.

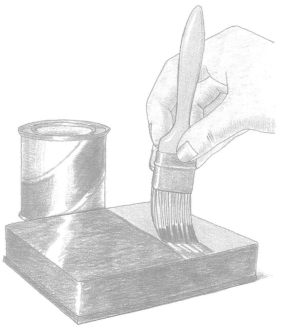

Paint effects are applied to the surface before adding the cut-out shapes.

### Household emulsion paint

Emulsion, which is available in a matt or silk finish, is a good base for découpage. Gloss household paint can also be used. Household emulsion does not come in a huge range of bright colours, but you can add colour pigment to white paint to obtain degrees of colour. Pots of craft matt emulsion colours can be bought in a good range of colours.

### Artists' acrylic paints

This paint comes in a wide range of colours and is quick drying. Mix it with water to dilute as necessary.

### Enamel paint

Small pots of model enamel paint can be used on wood as well as metal to produce a strong, hardwearing finish. It is available in matt as well as gloss finish.

### Metal paints

Various paints can be used on metal objects, from car spray paint to specialist metal paints in smooth or rough finishes.

### Spray paints

Polyurethane spray paints are a quick way to obtain a tough finish. Some surfaces will need to be sealed with a spray primer before painting it.

If the spray nozzle becomes clogged, remove the nozzle and run a knife blade through the slit in the stem. Then clear the nozzle itself with a pin.

## ADHESIVES FOR DECOUPAGE
### PVA adhesive

This is the main adhesive to use with découpage. To seal items before applying the cut-out shapes, dilute the PVA to the consistency of thin cream and paint all over the surface, then leave to dry. PVA can also be used as a varnish. Once the cut-out shapes have been applied, simply paint all over with a slightly diluted version of PVA and leave to dry.

### Wallpaper paste

This is very useful as it makes the paper very pliable so it can be moulded round awkward shapes. However, it can stretch some papers out of shape.

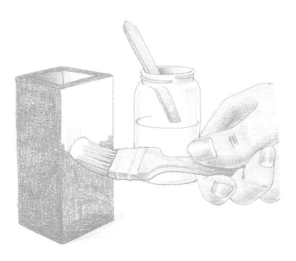

Paint the whole surface with dilute PVA adhesive, then leave to dry.

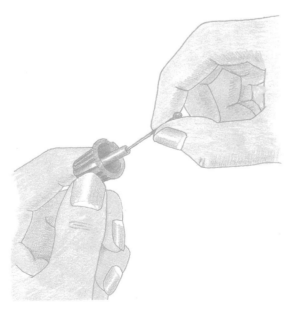

If a nozzle becomes clogged, clear it with the pointed end of a pin.

### Spray adhesive

Always use this adhesive when working with foil papers on glass (as in glass découpage) as they cannot absorb other adhesives. Use spray adhesive to make thin papers more durable by laminating them to a thicker paper for 3-D découpage. It can also be used to hold stencils in place while adding the paint.

## Clear adhesive
Clear, quick drying adhesive is a good multi-purpose glue to use with either card or paper shapes.

## Stick adhesive
This type of adhesive comes in a roll-up tube and is easy to control. It is a gentle adhesive that will not damage the paper.

## Self-adhesive stickers
Small self-adhesive stickers are used to separate the different layers of paper when creating a 3-D découpage motif.

## Temporary adhesive
Putty-like adhesive (Blu-tak) is used to hold the shapes temporarily in place while you decide on the design. It is especially useful in glass découpage when paper shapes are held inside a glass object.

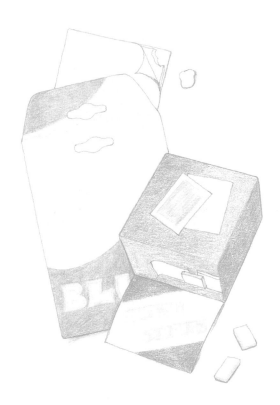

# REMOVING ADHESIVES
Adhesive manufacturers will always help with advice about solvents for their products and some do supply this in stores, where the adhesives are sold.

The first step for removing a blob of glue is to scrape off any deposit and then proceed as follows:

## Clear adhesive
On skin, wash first then remove any residue with nail varnish remover. On fabric, hold a pad of absorbent rag on the underside and dab on the right side with non-oily nail varnish.

## Epoxy adhesive
Lighter fuel or cellulose thinners will remove adhesive from the hands. On fabrics, hold a rag pad under the stain and dab with cellulose thinners on the right side. On synthetic fibre, use lighter fuel.

## Adhesive tape residue
White spirit or cellulose thinners may do it. Or try nail varnish remover.

## Latex adhesive
Lift off as much as possible before the adhesive hardens. Keep the adhesive soft with cold water and rub with a cloth. Treat any stains with liquid dry cleaner. Scrape off any deposits with a pencil eraser.

## Wallpaper paste
Scrape as much paste from the fabric as possible. Spread the fabric over a bowl or dish and pour cold water through the residue. Dab cold water on any remaining stain.

Putty-like adhesive (Blu-tak) and self-adhesive stickers can be used for securing cut-out shapes.

## EQUIPMENT
### Brushes
Household paint brushes can be used for applying paints and varnishes to items. Use children's craft brushes for applying adhesive and fine artists' brushes for delicate painting. Try to keep the brushes for each medium separate to prevent any discolouring. Clean brushes immediately after use, using water for water-based paints and white spirit for varnish.

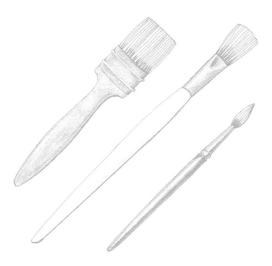

Use household paint brushes, children's craft brushes and fine artists' brushes.

### Hole punches
Hole punches are a useful addition to découpage equipment as they can be used to create perfect circles of paper or foil.

### Glasspaper
Glasspaper is available in a variety of grades from extremely fine to very coarse. Use coarser grades for rubbing down surfaces before painting. If several layers of varnish are used over the découpaged shapes, use a fine glasspaper to gently sand down in between the final coats.

### Masking tape
Masking tape can be combined with rough off-cuts of paper to mask off areas when using spray paints.

### Scissors
Two main types of scissors are used for découpage. When cutting out the delicate shapes for découpage, use a small pair of

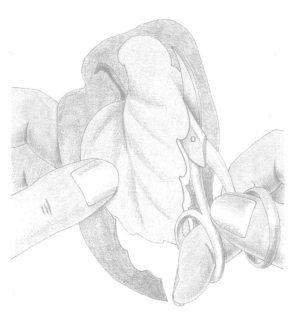

Use curved manicure scissors for cutting round delicate shapes.

curved manicure scissors. Large, sharp-pointed scissors can be used first to isolate a particular motif.

### Craft knives
When cutting straight edges, use a craft knife or scalpel against a metal ruler.

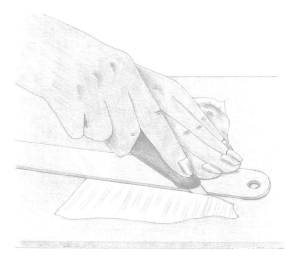

To cut straight edges, use a sharp craft knife or scalpel against a metal ruler.

## BASIC TECHNIQUES

As with any art or craft, before you begin check that you have all the materials and equipment that you need. Work with a cutting mat to hand for cutting with a craft knife and cover the surface with rough paper off-cuts or newspaper when using paint and varnish.

### Planning a design

The best thing about découpage is that you do not need to be able to draw to achieve a stunning result: the composition of any design is the placement of the cut-out shapes.

Before you begin, decide how you want the finished item to look. This will give you some idea of the type of paper you need to use to achieve this result. Lay the paper out on a flat surface and decide which part of the design you want to use, then cut out the shapes.

Once you have an array of cut-out shapes, arrange them into an attractive design.

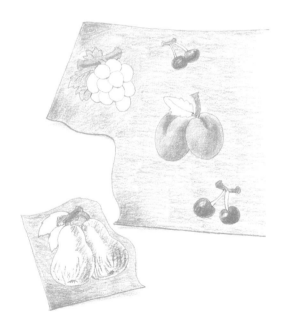

Lay the paper on a flat surface and decide which part of the design you want to use.

The shapes do not need to be cut out individually; for example, groups of flowers can be cut out together. Once you have an array of cut-out shapes on a flat surface, you can arrange them into a design. The item that you are découpaging will help you make the

decision when planning the arrangement as it will dictate the amount of surface on which you can place the shapes.

Once you are happy with the design, either draw round the shapes on a plain sheet of paper and use this as a guide when securing the real thing, or use putty adhesive (Blu-tack) to hold the shapes temporarily in position on the object you are decorating and remove it as you stick each shape firmly in place. If you are not confident about your design skills, just cut out as many shapes as you can and simply cover the whole item, arranging the cut-out shapes in straight rows or overlapping them in a random effect.

### Fixing the papers

If you are unsure of any of the papers you are using, or the paper is two-sided, spray over the whole sheet on both sides with fixative and leave to dry before you cut out the shapes. This will provide the paper with a protective surface and also stop the paper from turning yellow with age.

### Preparing different surfaces

Once the cut-out shapes are in place the item will simply be varnished. If you want a different or unusual paint finish on the item, this must be done before the shapes are stuck down.

Rub the surface of the item to remove any old paint or varnish, or to simply smooth down a new surface. Wipe away the dust with a damp cloth. On glass and ceramic pieces, just make sure that the surfaces are clean and free from grease.

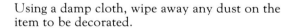

Using a damp cloth, wipe away any dust on the item to be decorated.

### Cutting out the shapes

Lay out the paper and choose which motifs you want to use. Roughly cut out each motif with large scissors, leaving a good margin all round.

Change to small curved manicure scissors and carefully cut round the

outline. On shapes where the outline is unclear either use a soft pencil to mark in a line to follow or gently curve the cutting line to give an attractive edge to the shape. Hold the scissor blades at a slight angle away from you as you cut round a shape. By cutting the paper at an angle you create a bevelled edge, making the heavy cutting line less obvious.

Use a sharp craft knife or a scalpel and a metal ruler to cut straight edges. Use straight blades and keep changing them as damaged blades will drag the paper rather than cutting it. Always cut on a special cutting mat so as not to ruin the working surface.

Use a set square and ruler to check right angles and parallel lines. Line up the straight metal edge against the line to be cut. Press the craft knife against the metal edge and firmly draw the knife towards you, keeping an even pressure on the straight edge to keep it still.

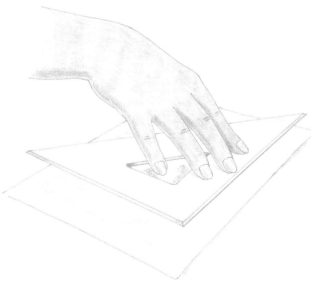

Use a set square and ruler to check right angles and parallel lines.

If the paper is thick, score the cutting line gently to mark it, then, still with the straight edge in position, cut along the line again, pressing harder on the craft knife to cut through the paper.

To cut round curves, mark the shape lightly with the knife point and cut round making sure that the free hand is pressing firmly on the paper to keep it still, but out of the way of the knife's path. To cut small shapes with right angles and tight curves, start by piercing the corner point of each shape with the point of the blade and cut away from the corner, drawing the knife towards you. This should ensure neatly cut points.

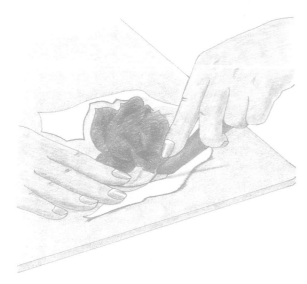

To cut right angles and tight curves, pierce the paper and draw the knife towards you.

To cut curves, use the free hand to press firmly on the paper, but out of the knife's path.

Alternatively, paper can be torn into strips or small pieces. When you tear a piece of paper along its grain the paper rips easily and the torn edge is fairly even. Paper torn across the grain leaves a jagged edge which can be attractive, but it is more difficult to control the torn edge.

**Sticking the shapes in place**
Apply a layer of adhesive to the back of the shape (in glass découpage the adhesive is applied to the front) with a paint brush, making sure that the whole shape has been covered. Use tweezers to pick up tiny glued shapes. Lay the shapes over the item and gently smooth in place with your fingers and a damp cloth to eliminate air bubbles and excess adhesive. Once the shapes are in the correct position, check that they are firmly stuck together. If a piece is loose, use a cocktail stick to slip some adhesive under the paper edge.

To keep fingers clean, use tweezers to pick up tiny sticky shapes.

**Varnishing**
Traditionally, découpage had up to 20 layers of varnish over the cut-out shapes, so the edges of the shapes merged into the background. However with today's varnishes, with good total coverage, only 8–10 coats are now necessary.